one another

love

one another

how to let God's heart shine
through your life

gloria chisholm

WATERBROOK
PRESS

LOVE ONE ANOTHER
PUBLISHED BY WATERBROOK PRESS
5446 North Academy Boulevard, Suite 200
Colorado Springs, Colorado 80918
A division of Random House, Inc.

Some of the stories in this book are composites of several different situations; details and names have been changed to protect identities.

Scripture taken from the *Holy Bible, New International Version*®. NIV® Copyright © 1973, 1978, 1984 by the International Bible Society. Used by permission of Zondervan Publishing House. All rights reserved.

ISBN 1-57856-310-0

Library of Congress Cataloging-in-Publication Data
Chisholm, Gloria, 1951–
    Love one another : how to let God's heart shine through your life / Gloria Chisholm.— 1st ed.
        p.   cm.
    Includes bibliographical references.
    ISBN 1-57856-310-0
        1. Love—Religious aspects—Christianity.   2. God—Love.   I. Title.

 BV4639.C484   2000
 241'.4—dc21

                                                                        00-022846

Printed in the United States of America
2000—First Edition

10 9 8 7 6 5 4 3 2 1

To Barb

contents

acknowledgments

I want to thank my agents, Andrew Whelchel and Jason Cangialosi, for their loyalty, support, constant encouragement, and, most of all, their belief in me as a writer and as a person.

I hardly know how to express my gratitude to my editor, Liz Heaney, who is also my friend. Wrestling together with many of the concepts of love and forgiveness has made both of us, I think, better people and has given us a deeper understanding of what it means to live in the world as authentic lovers and forgivers. She has helped me reach for the God-given wisdom inside of myself that I didn't even know was there.

Finally, I'm grateful to all of you "out there" who have taught me how to love and forgive. You've been so patient as I took bumbling baby steps, walking all over many of your toes in the process, while you acted as if you hardly noticed. Thank you.

introduction

As a young mother I thought I knew a lot about love. I'd been a Christian for several years, memorized a lot of scripture, prayed daily, served my church and community. But then our six-year-old neighbor girl ran over my three-year-old son's leg with her bike and snapped it in two. Leaving my screaming son on her driveway, she threw her bike down and ran inside. Her mother never came outside to see what the fuss was all about, and once they found out what happened, none of the family ever called to see how Dwight was doing. They never even spoke to us again. Until then they'd been quite friendly.

"God, how do I love this family?" I remember praying fervently.

Then I met a woman whose mother and daughter were killed by a drunk driver. And I thought *my* situation was challenging. She recalls the accident: "When I heard they had both died in the crash, a scream rose up from the center of the earth and came out through my mouth."

Yet she somehow found within her (I can't imagine how) compassion and love for the drunk driver. A few months later she wrote the woman a letter, forgiving her. They now correspond regularly. Where does that kind of love come from?

No ready answer comes to mind. We can't explain in simple words where God's kind of love comes from. But I do believe that if we honestly wrestle with our questions about love, God will reveal his answers—answers as individual as we are, as unique as the circumstances we face each day of our lives. If we can commit to wrestling, the answers will appear.

As we think about how we can truly love the people in our world, a good place to start might be to make a list of everything we already know about love. Of course, that might be a very short list; how much do we really *know* about this subject?

Let me rephrase my suggestion. Let's make a list of everything we've ever *heard* or *been taught* about love. Go ahead, take a piece of paper and write it down—sermons you've heard, books you've read, movies you've seen, scriptures you've memorized, whatever—anything you can remember ever hearing about love. Things such as:

- God is love
- Love feels good
- Love hurts
- Love means never having to say you're sorry
- Love never lasts

Now you can throw away your list. It's not what we know or think we know or what we've been taught about love that matters, that makes us who we are. A list of what we believe about love may simply reflect our wounds from past relationships—or our joys if love's been good to us. Our list may just be an itemizing of what we believe in our heads. It may have nothing at all to do with our hearts.

If love doesn't have anything to do with our experiences or

what we've been taught, then what *does* it have to do with? It has to do with how we live our lives every day as children of the God of love. You see, we are made in God's image (Genesis 1:27). It's the first thing on record that God tells us about ourselves. Furthermore, while "no one has ever seen God...if we love one another, God lives in us and his love is made complete in us" (1 John 4:12). In other words, when we are loving, the world is seeing the image of God in us.

This book is about living God's kind of love—out loud and in living color. Love is not what you *feel* for your kids or partner or other loved ones, although feelings certainly play a part. Love is what you *do*, who you *are*, how you relate to others—out there. Are you allowing God to express himself through you? Are you an example of God's image in your relationships with others? Are you letting love drive your actions and relationships—everything that you do and are in a given day? My challenge to you, as you read the following pages, is that you commit to love one another deeply, from the heart (see 1 Peter 1:22).

It takes twenty-one days to form a habit. If you read a chapter per day, pondering the questions and doing the exercises, after three weeks you'll have a good start on loving your world.

If you can do so honestly and with conviction, I suggest you consciously make the following commitment before reading another word:

> *I commit to love my world—deeply and from my heart— every day, every hour, every minute of every day.*

On the last page of this book you'll be given the opportunity to make your commitment a vow to live by.

Chapter One

what the world
needs now

Juvenile homicides in America have increased more than two and one-half times since 1984.

One in three black Americans lives in poverty.

One in four women in America is diagnosed each year as clinically depressed. (Speaking of depression, I read that a recent $1.5 million study by researchers at Carnegie Mellon University found that those who spend even a few hours a week on-line experience higher levels of depression and loneliness than they would have if they used the computer network less frequently. Progress. Interesting.)[1]

And these problems are just one small drop in the proverbial bucket of troubles we face in our country alone. It would seem to me that the world is still missing some particular ingredient in the recipe for a rich and satisfying life. Unfortunately, that missing ingredient often eludes us.

We all want it. We all need it. Many of us don't know how to go about getting it, at least in healthy ways, and so the real thing continues to elude us. And if we can't get it, we can't give it.

Or so we've been told.

But what about Erica, a twenty-five-year-old woman, who was interviewed recently on *Prime Time*? The first time *Prime Time* interviewed her, Erica was fourteen and had just run away from her home where her father sexually abused her and her mother did nothing to stop it.

"It's okay, I can handle myself out here," she had said with a careless shrug of her shoulders. "Everybody wants something from you, you know. You learn to survive."

My heart broke to hear the toughness in her voice, to see it in her demeanor, the toughness she had to wear like a cloak to protect herself from the predators she probably encountered just about every day on the streets.

And then the camera focused on a group of men, young and old, gathered around a table playing a game of some kind. An older, softer Erica sat in the middle of them. "Dan, it's not kind to talk when other people are talking," she spoke gently to the young man sitting next to her. "When he's done, then it's your turn." She turned to another young man across the table. "Do you want another cookie, Steve?"

Erica now works with the mentally disabled. By offering to others the compassion, guidance, and kindness she never received as a child, she is loving her world.

I know of a pastor who was abandoned as a child by his father, but he now leads an inner-city church that gives timelessly to the homeless, to those suffering with AIDS, and to the mentally ill. He, too, is loving his world despite his childhood.

One of the most loving people I have ever known, my friend Carol, was raised by a tyrannical father and an alcoholic mother. She was taking care of her baby brother when she was only six years old because there was no one else to do it. Today she opens her home to young girls who need to talk, who need someone to confide in, who are troubled in their relationships with their parents. She holds group meetings with these girls once a week and also teaches a weekly Bible study for hurting women. Even more important, she's a loving wife to her husband of thirty years, sticking by him through a midlife crisis when he moved from job to job and staying committed to her marriage when the stress of their teenage daughter's death from a brain tumor threatened the very fiber of their union. Carol may not have received a lot of love as a child, but she is a living example that love truly is a choice. She is redeeming her childhood wounds and making up for the lack in how she herself was parented.

So is it true we can only love others if we ourselves have been loved? What does it mean to be loved? What if our parents loved us the best they could, but since their love fell far short of our insatiable need, we perceived that we weren't loved at all? Does this mean they didn't love us?

We can ask the same questions about our relationship with God. Is the depth of God's love for us determined by our ability to believe and/or receive his love? Does God love us because we are lovable? Or because God is love?

I ask these questions to get us thinking about love and about our commitment to love our world in the light of these words: "Dear children, let us not love with words or tongue but with actions and in truth" (1 John 3:18). If there is an answer to all of the above questions, I believe it can be found a little further on in

7

the book of 1 John: "We love because he first loved us" (4:19). Not because our parents loved us perfectly. Not because we *feel* loved by our spouse, children, or friends. Not because the world has treated us well.

Why do we love? Because God loves us.

This should come as a relief. We don't have to go through years of therapy, identifying every dysfunction in our family of origin, in order to love our world. We don't have to memorize all the scriptures in the Bible on love. We don't even have to understand this thing called love. We only have to *acknowledge* God's love for us and then, with God's help, simply *decide* to love others "with actions and in truth."

Because we don't always feel it, acknowledging God's love is sometimes a step of faith. This has been true for me. On the verge of a divorce from my husband of thirteen years, the reality that I would soon be a single parent of five children was beginning to sink in. I felt more pain and more terror than I'd ever known. All of my dreams for an intact family, a happy home, and a secure foundation for my kids were crumbling. And I held God responsible. If he cared about us, he never would have let this happen.

I called my pastor's wife one day, crying out with the agony of it all. I poured out my heart and then, finally, I whimpered, "I know somehow I have to believe God loves me."

"But you don't *feel* loved, do you?" she asked quietly.

No. I definitely didn't feel loved. I felt betrayed, rejected, abandoned. But I'd learned so much about God's character over the years, and everything I'd learned pointed to the fact that he was a God of love. So somewhere down deep I believed he loved me. Not feeling loved, I was beginning to learn, didn't mean I wasn't loved. By God or by others.

The knowledge that God loved me in spite of my feelings gave me the courage and the will to begin to reach outside of myself to love a world that, like me, didn't always feel God's love and care. Maybe there was a way I could communicate God's love, even in the midst of my despair over my broken marriage. That day, out of my own need, I began to write my book *Encourage One Another*. I knew somehow I wasn't alone in my desperate need for love and encouragement. I wanted to write a book that would offer redemptive answers to those who were suffering the kind of pain I was. *Encourage One Another* showed readers that it is possible to reach out in love, to comfort others, to heal—even in the midst of great trauma. Even when we don't feel loved ourselves.

Our culture has programmed us to believe that love is a feeling. We hear this message on the radio, read it in romance novels, and watch it on the movie screen. And I'll be the first to admit that when a warm, cuddly feeling accompanies a loving action, the whole experience is much more enjoyable.

However, love is often more like plowing a field than it is like snuggling with a loved one. I've done both, and—okay, I'm not an expert; I've only driven a tractor once—I can tell you plowing isn't nearly as much fun as snuggling.

But loving someone isn't about having fun with that person—though it can be. It isn't about warm, cuddly feelings—though it can be that, too.

No, love is about God's reaching out his arms to a hurting and lonely world through human beings. You. Me. Depending on one's individual gifts, love can take the form of a German chocolate cake or a cure for cancer.

Love is about commitment, a commitment (1) to see people through the eyes of Christ so that we can refrain from making human judgments and condemning them for what we don't like or don't understand about them, and (2) to reach redemptively into the world with all the truth we've received in Jesus Christ so we can walk in integrity and authenticity.

Love.

It's what the world needs now.

It's all we have to give.

Will you join me in making a commitment to be a part of the action—God's redemptive action in people's hearts?

Ask Yourself

Am I convinced that the world needs love now? If so, where do I fit into the picture?

Did I feel loved as a child? Does it matter? Have I worked through my childhood issues to the point that I can now reach out to love others?

What resources, either inside or outside of myself, do I still need to access in order to give me the desire, the courage, and the strength to give up any self-absorption and make loving my world a priority?

Can I simply make a decision to do what I don't necessarily feel like doing?

What would that look like in practical application?

To Do

Write your mission statement—a simple statement of purpose that clearly unveils your promise to love your world. Be as specific as you can; list at least five gifts/talents/abilities you feel capable of and confident about sharing with others.

1. Amy Harmon, "Study Links Internet and Depression," *Seattle Times*, 30 August 1998. Published originally in the *New York Times*.

Chapter Two

love's criteria

We don't usually wake up one day and decide that this is the day we're going to start loving our world. Oh, the decision may be made in one day, but a lot can happen before we arrive at that place.

In my case, I had developed an ever-increasing tendency to self-protect, to wear a "suit of armor" whenever I interacted with others—strangers and loved ones alike, but mostly loved ones. Loved ones, after all, can hurt us the most. In order to ensure that no one inflicted a fresh wound, I refused to be vulnerable with others. Not only did this take a tremendous amount of energy each day, it also kept love out—God's and everyone else's.

Part of what woke me up to my turtlelike behavior was thinking about my mother—now gone—who had received some blows early in her life and never let God redeem them. At the end of her life, she had little capacity either to give or receive love. She was hardened. Bitter. Alone.

The image of my mother finally scared me into a conversation

13

about all of this. "Okay, I'm a closed person," I admitted to a friend one day. "So what am I supposed to do?"

Some months before, my friend had taken it upon herself to try to convince me of God's love for me—even though I'd been a Christian for many years, I didn't have that down. Now she just looked at me. "Well, for starters," she began, filing her nails as if this were a casual conversation about the weather rather than a personal crisis that could affect my life forever, "I'm no longer going to talk to you about God's love—"

"What? Why—"

"—until you open your heart," she went on. "Your heart is closed, and nothing is getting through. I'm wasting my breath, my time—"

"So what's a little breath and time?" I argued. "My entire spiritual journey's at stake here, the kind of person I'm becoming..." She was my biggest cheerleader. If she quit...

She shook her head. "It's up to you."

"Okay, okay, I'll open up." I said it grudgingly, like a child waiting for the awful-tasting medicine that will soon permeate every corner of her mouth but is supposed to heal her cold or something.

It was all God needed to hear. Something began to happen in my heart the very moment that I exercised my will. I don't even know if I had a will before that. I had heard about God's love. I'd read about it in the Bible. I believed that he probably loved some of the folks on the planet. But when I chose to open my heart that day I began to *know* his love for me. I *knew* it was there when I screwed up, I *knew* it was there when I was afraid, I *knew* it was there whether I felt it on an emotional level or not.

And so, in turn, because "God first loved me," I began to love others. Not overnight, but little by little a deep knowledge of God's love for me began to spill out to those around me. I couldn't help it.

If you want to commit to being a lover in your world, only two things are required. First, you must exercise your will to open your heart to fully receive God's love (Psalm 51:12 and 2 Corinthians 6:13), no matter what happened in your past that caused you to close up. Second, you must solicit God's help (Isaiah 58:9) when the ability to love seems out of your control.

Consider the first criterion for a moment. Those of us who have experienced deep emotional wounds gradually close up—to God and to others—in order to protect ourselves from further assaults. We may not even realize how closed we are; we still attend church, pray, get together with friends. But we withhold something important, something that's meant to be shared. We withhold ourselves. We close ourselves off from others; we refuse to be vulnerable.

Look around you. You'll see closed people and open people, and whether or not they are Christians has little to do with it. Even when we become Christians, many of us withhold certain parts of ourselves from God and others. Some, but certainly not all, indications of a closed person are a stiff walk, a tight jaw, clipped words and fast sentences, nervous behavior, a negative attitude, and a rigid belief system. On the other hand, some indications of an open person are a welcoming smile, gentle words, relaxed behavior, genuine optimism, vulnerability, and a grateful heart.

I was definitely a closed person. You, too, may find that you're closed and need to open up. I hate to be the one to tell you this; it can be such a painful process, especially if, like me, you've been closed for a long time. But the truth is we can reach out to love our world only when we open up and allow God's love to permeate every corner of our own heart.

As for the second criterion, do you think you're going to be able to love all of the weird people on the planet all by yourself? What about that annoying loudmouth in your office? Or that bratty kid down the street who keeps bullying your child? Or your obnoxious mother-in-law who won't stay out of your family business? Remember—we want to make loving our world a *daily* thing, and these kinds of people, not to mention the child molesters, Saddam Husseins, and wife-beaters of the world, seem to keep popping up everywhere, testing the limits of our ability to love. But when we just can't muster it up, we don't have to feel guilty—we only have to be able to scream, "God! Help!"

That's all it takes. Two things: an exercising of your will to open your heart and the ability to scream, "Help!"

That's within the realm of possibility, isn't it?

Ask Yourself

Can I meet the criteria for becoming God's lover in my world? How can I exercise my will to love today?

As I consider the lives of those I touch on a regular basis, do I feel a scream coming on? How can I get out of the way and allow God to help me love those whom I have no capability within myself to love?

To Do

Consider where you might need God's help—opening up, exercising your will, loving a certain person or persons. Confess your need to at least one person who will hold you accountable. Assure yourself with the promise in Isaiah 58:9: "Then you will call, and the LORD will answer; you will cry for help, and he will say: Here am I."

"Here am I." What powerful and wonderfully comforting words.

Chapter Three

loving yourself

When my children were small, I made a conscious decision to always greet them in the morning with a big smile and a bigger hug. That way, they were guaranteed that at least once a day someone would be happy—ecstatic even—to see them. (My children all have attention deficit disorder. Many teachers and some of their classmates were less than happy to see them enter a room.)

"Good morning, Grant!" I'd say with a smile as I flipped pancakes on the griddle. "I'm so glad to see you." And as the others trailed in, with tousled hair and wiping the sleep out of their eyes, "Good morning Travis, Dwight, Merilee." And, finally, the littlest. "Oh, and there's my Amber."

I did this for years, although I might have become less enthusiastic as the preteen years approached. But I kept making the effort. It was the least I could do to get their day off to a loving start.

If you're a parent, you have loving routines of your own that you engage in with your kids. So why is it so difficult, not usually even occurring to us, that we owe the same kind of morning greeting to ourselves? If we want to love others, we first need to love ourselves.

A certain Pharisee, trying to test Jesus, asked him one day, "Teacher, which is the greatest commandment in the Law?" After telling the Pharisee that first of all he should love the Lord his God, Jesus said a strange thing: "And the second [commandment] is like it: 'Love your neighbor as yourself'" (see Matthew 22:36-39).

Love my neighbor as myself? Was Jesus forgetting that I go around a lot of the time calling myself a dork because of some stupid thing I did? Or that I'm always kicking myself because of some inappropriate thing I said? Or that I'm impatient with myself because I can't seem to control my impulses? If I'm to love my neighbor as I love myself, I'm afraid my neighbor is in big trouble. Why? Because to the degree that we love ourselves, to that degree do we love others. Likewise, to the degree that we judge and condemn ourselves, to that degree do we judge and condemn others.

I write to an inmate in our state prison. In a recent letter, he told me how he had become a cynic, tough, not caring about anyone or anything, least of all himself. Later, in that same letter, he projected that same judgment onto others. "No one cares, and I refuse to make myself vulnerable to everyone else's madness." Obviously, someone, maybe many someones, had hurt him very deeply at some point in his life. He sees no value in relationships because he believes he has nothing to give. Where do you begin with someone like that? I started a letter back to him but almost gave up in despair when I realized the enormity of my task—to convince a man who spends twenty-one out of twenty-four hours of every day alone in an eight-foot-by-twelve-foot cell that his life has value and that if he could discover God's love for him, he might in turn love others. Everything I believe about this love stuff suddenly seemed shallow and void. Why should he believe me?

Yet I know that until this man recognizes and acknowledges that he is deeply loved by God and can therefore love himself, it will be difficult, maybe impossible for him, to see any value in his life at all. And while I know I'm not responsible for the wounds he's received in his life up until now, I do believe that I can be a part of his healing, that if I can stick this out and be a consistent source of God's love to him, constantly reminding him that his life is of priceless worth, he can find the kind of self-love that will enable him to reach outside of himself to love others. And he needs to get on it; there are a lot of folks where he lives who need his love.

How well do *you* love yourself? What does it mean to love yourself? We're taught, even as children, to put others first, ourselves last. When we accepted Christ, this principle became even more ingrained in us. Added to that, the church seems to focus on our sinfulness, often neglecting to balance that fact with the biblical truth that we're also made in God's image—pretty special. No wonder we have a little problem with loving ourselves. It's been only in the last few years that I've begun to understand the kind of love Jesus was talking about in Matthew 22. It's not about putting ourselves first and others last, but about making self-love (nurturing the self) a priority so that we have the inner resources to love others when the opportunity presents itself.

If the young inmate had written me his letter a few years ago, I would have immediately commiserated with him: "Yeah, I know what you mean, no one cares, it's awful the way people love you and leave you, yada, yada, yada..." At that particular time in my life I, too, wondered where God was. Only after I finally realized that God loves *me* did I have any love within me to give my friend.

How do we make self-love a priority? We first have to stop and listen to our hearts, our bodies, our minds. We have to *know* ourselves.

It may mean spending some time with God and yourself first thing in the morning before you go out into the world. It may mean leaving a tense meeting at work to step out into the hall and take some deep breaths. It may even sometimes mean saying no to your child's request to read him a story. I can hear you now: "But that's selfish. I wouldn't think of saying no—" And therein lies part of our problem. We never say no. We pride ourselves on it. But we eventually burn out, become resentful of anyone's requests, get cranky, feel guilty for our feelings, then excuse them by saying we have PMS, or we're in a midlife crisis, or whatever—all of which we could have avoided simply by listening to ourselves and honoring our own needs along the way. If only we could have loved ourselves better.

By the way, saying no to our kids sometimes and being honest about the reason models behavior they will need someday when society pressures them to keep moving faster—too fast to stop and remember that they need to love themselves. In fact, saying no to *anyone* in order to better love and take care of ourselves is modeling godly self-love.

We've made a commitment to love our world. And if we're going to love our world, we have to learn to love ourselves. I find that Galatians 5:22-23 is the perfect yardstick to measure how well we're loving ourselves: "But the fruit of the Spirit is love, joy, peace, patience, kindness, goodness, faithfulness, gentleness and self-control." How well are we applying the fruit of the Spirit to our relationship with ourselves?

Ask Yourself

What's keeping me from loving myself?

What have I been taught about my worth and value—by my parents and siblings, by the church?

What is one thing I can do for myself today that will spill over to my world?

To Do

Apply Philippians 4:8 by making a list of all of the qualities you love about yourself. Post it somewhere you can see it. Read this list at least once a day for twenty-one days. Also, look for these qualities in others, and affirm them whenever you can.

Chapter Four

conscious loving

To consider what it means to love consciously, we must assume it's possible to love *un*consciously. I suspect that we love unconsciously because we *live* unconsciously. We go about our daily lives without really thinking or being intentional.

Living unconsciously can be compared to sleepwalking; we're awake in that we're walking around, but we're not conscious of what we're doing or why. If asked, we would say we love the people in our lives—but we're not awake to that love, to what it means, to its depth. We claim that we love others because the Bible says we should, because it would be a sin not to love a spouse or a child or a parent, because, well, we have to face these people every day and if we ever showed our true feelings, we might not have anyone left to love. As far as the teenagers hanging around the 7-Eleven or our dentist or the bad driver in front of us, of course we love them, too. They're part of the world, and aren't we supposed to love everyone?

But can you picture, for a moment, a sleepwalker? How conscious do you think that person is of loving you or anyone else? If you ask him, he may repeat the words, "I love you." But he's in a trance. Do those words mean anything?

Unconscious loving (and living) can take on many forms:

- A husband and wife who stay in their dead marriage because "God hates divorce." They're outwardly polite to one another, but they don't face the internal issues that caused the breakdown of the marriage. They are simply existing together.

- Siblings who can't stand each other because of unresolved childhood issues, but who never deal with the root cause of their rivalry; as children, they lived together, and as adults, they come together at family gatherings only because they have to. They make small talk, play board games, share meals, but make no effort to reach one another's heart.

- Two friends who get together regularly but who never think about or discuss the friendship itself or their feelings for one another. They engage in surface conversations rather than reach down inside themselves for feelings and the meaning buried somewhere in their shallow discussions.

Another form of unconscious loving takes place with those we don't know but may claim in some broad sense to "love": the homeless man we toss a dollar to, the other children we see every day when we drop our own kids off at day care, and the janitor who cleans our office every night, to name just a few. Do we even *see* these people, let alone stop to love them, whatever that looks like in our busy day?

When my children were small, I tried to love them consciously most of the time. I read them stories, took them to the park, and put Band-Aids on their owies, not because I was a mother and that's what mothers do, but because I enjoyed doing things for and with them. I *wanted* to do these things.

But somewhere along the way, it stopped being fun. Everything became much more complicated than reading stories and going to the park together, and at that point, my own "owies" seemed more important than my children's. I never stopped loving my kids, but my own wounds were surfacing and demanding my attention. However, I wasn't ready to give them my attention; instead, I moved into a state of numbness. I stopped feeling the acute pain, but I also stopped feeling love for others. My loving became unconscious. I stopped *seeing* my kids. Oh, sometimes I saw them, but what I saw was a mass of little people all demanding something from me. I would put lunches together but had no energy for the love notes I once enclosed in lunchboxes. I would help them with homework but forget to praise them when they did well. I would show up at soccer games and school assemblies, but my mind was on how I was going to pay a certain bill or how I could escape for a weekend getaway.

Then one day I began to see the consequences of my Rip Van Winkle sleep: I was losing connection with both myself and my kids. Even in my stupor, I knew that when we lose those vital connections, we don't always make it back.

I became conscious about loving my kids once again but in a different way because now my motivation did not come from my children's smiling faces, hugs, kisses, and "Mommy, I love you's." My teenagers, while still responsive to me, were in trouble. My only reward was the simple knowledge of two things: (1) my teenagers and I were maintaining a relational connection, and (2) God was pleased that I was still putting effort, while meager at times, into my role as "Mommy."

Conscious loving, then, is not necessarily connected to how it feels to love a particular person. When we have fallen asleep, for whatever reason, and then one day begin to wake up, the feelings do gradually return. That is one way we know we're waking up. But the feelings may not always be loving ones. When we're unconscious, we're numb. When we wake up, we may feel anger, resentment, or annoyance before we arrive at care, empathy, compassion, and finally love. Agape love.

First John 3:18 says, "Dear children, let us…love…with actions and in truth." This really makes it all so simple, when you think about it. The definition of *conscious* loving is *active and honest* loving. The three relational scenarios just summarized serve as good examples of unconscious loving; they are neither active nor honest. Conscious loving takes an act of our will. We make a decision to love with action and in truth. We can be confident we are doing God's will, regardless of how we feel during the process of loving someone, and even regardless of the outcome of our actions.

I remember the day I sat across from one of my young adult children in an Italian restaurant and said: "I care about your needs, your problems, your life, but I can't listen anymore to your blaming and accusations, as if everything that has ever happened to you is my fault. I know I've done some stuff wrong, and I'm so sorry, but your attacks are wearing me down."

I said these words after months, maybe even years, of listening, validating feelings, apologizing for any hurt I'd caused. But I had finally become aware that I'd done all I could do, and now my daughter needed to take some responsibility, to own her feelings, to do some of her own grief work, to start the forgiveness and healing process. I sensed strongly that this was the next step God wanted us to take in our relationship and that my daughter had to personally take responsibility for her own growth. I held my breath and waited for her response.

I didn't have long to wait. My daughter almost upended the table in the outburst that followed. Screaming. Hateful words. Running from the restaurant. And I was left alone at the table, my untouched ravioli suddenly not the least bit appetizing.

I had no contact with my child for three weeks. There were times when I wondered if I'd done the loving thing, if I'd loved her well at the restaurant. Still, while I felt grief and some anxiety over the break in our relationship, wondering whether my child would ultimately forgive me or choose to keep blaming me, deep down I knew I had loved with action and truth at that moment of confrontation.

I'd stayed current with my feelings for this child along the way so that when the confrontation took place, I was already at a place of compassion, even though my words might not have sounded compassionate to her. I hoped she'd do some internal work of her own. When we did finally talk, I continued to affirm my love and care, and the difficult confrontation in the restaurant became a turning point in our relationship. My child ended up taking some personal responsibility, which led to more dialogue, which led ultimately to one of the most honest relationships I've ever had. This child and I are now close and very much in touch with feelings of love for one another. Without the confrontation she would never have had to examine her real feelings for me. She could have kept on loving me unconsciously forever, and while we might have been polite on the surface, our relationship wouldn't have been real.

It's awesome—what can happen when we are committed to consciously loving our world, whether a spouse, a child, a friend, a neighbor, or even an enemy.

Conscious loving is about being alert to those moments God nudges us and says, "Now." Awake to those times when God may push us rather forcefully, it feels, into the front lines of something akin to a war, as he did in the confrontation with my daughter. Awake to those opportunities that come along once in a lifetime, where loving is truly a privilege and an honor: to care for a child with Down syndrome, a friend dying of cancer, a pen pal on death row. These are noble assignments that require from us the most committed and conscious love of which we're capable.

It's up to each one of us just how consciously we choose to love the people God brings into our lives, how much time to spend on those relationships, what kind of love we put into them.

Do you want to love more consciously, to know when you are loving unconsciously? Wouldn't you like to wake up? Just a bit? To be a better lover? A lover of action and truth?

Ask Yourself

How can I become more conscious of how to love the people I live with and come in contact with today?

What is one way I can adjust my schedule today to include at least one conscious act of love?

To Do

Think about the people in your life. Which ones are you loving consciously? Unconsciously? Determine to perform a specific, conscious, loving act of integrity toward someone you're now pretty much taking for granted. Or choose a person you are not attracted to, someone you may even dislike or with whom you have a combative relationship, and do something loving. You may even choose to remain anonymous.

Chapter Five

loving creatively

Our pattern of loving can become a rut with grooves as deep as any we fall into—taking the same route to and from work, eating the same food day after day, seeing the same people over and over again. "Well, how bad can that be?" you ask. "If you gotta be in a rut, what could be better than that of the rut of loving?"

But the point is, you *don't* "gotta be in a rut." Loving can be—should be—an art. What makes our work art, whether we're loving or building a house, is the creativity we put into it. When we fall into a rut, any kind of rut, we are no longer involved in art. Our actions become rote, unconscious. The very definition of rut, according to Webster, is a "fixed routine procedure or course of action, thought, etc., especially one regarded as dull and unrewarding." The definition of art, on the other hand, is "creative work or its principles; making or doing of things that display form, beauty, and unusual perception."

We can't be creative when we're unconscious, wouldn't you agree?

I read recently of a woman in Manhattan who came up with a creative way to love her world. A volunteer nurse, she decided to raise money for a New York cancer center—through a chain letter. She sent a letter to ten friends asking them to mail ten dollars apiece to the cancer center, then forward the letter to ten others. And so on. In a year and a half, she raised eight hundred thousand dollars. So far. The money is still pouring in. Amazing.

Creative loving is simply going a bit out of your way, surprising others with kindness, moving beyond what is expected of you.

And I don't mean putting a bunch of sparkly confetti in your next card or letter to someone—the kind that falls into the recipient's lap and makes a big mess. That kind of surprise is neither kind nor loving. It's annoying (at least to people like me).

How about showing up at a friend's house on moving day with a pizza? Or washing a loved one's car for no good reason? Or throwing a surprise Valentine Day party for your child? An act of creative loving doesn't have to be something as big as raising money for cancer—unless that's what you feel God's calling you to on a particular day. The question to keep asking yourself is: How can I creatively love so-and-so today? And that's the key to loving creatively: being willing to be or do whatever God requires whenever he requires it.

In our last neighborhood, my two daughters somehow became engaged in a war of sorts with two sisters in a neighboring apartment. Every day my girls would come home with a report of exchanged insults and conflict between the two girls and themselves.

I could see things were escalating. Time for some creative love. But when I told the girls my idea, they were somewhat less than enthusiastic.

"What?" one of them shrieked. "You've got to be kidding!"

Her sister shook her head. "No way."

But I was still the mom. The boss. I paid the rent and all that. You know how it is. They had to do what I said. And so for a week straight, every single day, our project became loving our neighbors. Creatively. Tangibly. Anonymously. I wanted to teach my girls that acting in a loving way, even when one didn't feel loving, could actually change one's hateful feelings toward others. Besides, this is where I felt God was directing us; this particular relationship was the cutting edge for my girls at the moment. Everyone was stuck. It was up to them to do something creative to turn the tide.

The first day my girls had to find one nice item in their bedroom (the emphasis was on nice, as all in one piece, clean, new-looking), put it into a gift bag, and leave it on our neighbors' doorstep. The next day they had to find something in nature, the next day something they made with their own hands, and so on. All anonymously.

My daughters came home from school one day and reported: "Well, now Tam and Angela think someone's stalking them. We heard them telling some kids…"

Oh well. Creative loving doesn't guarantee positive results. That's not the point. The point is what my own daughters learned in the process of creative loving. They learned that:

- Creative love takes effort—they couldn't just throw any old thing together.
- Creative love decreases hateful feelings—they found themselves looking at the other girls a bit differently from then on.
- Creative love is its own reward—the girls actually

anticipated putting their gift together and sneaking up to our neighbors' porch each evening.

So how can you begin to love creatively?

You start by standing back to observe all of your relationships—old and new, healthy and not so healthy, close and distant, confidants and acquaintances. The purpose here is not to make you feel bad about the ruts many of your relationships have fallen into. Loving people is never bad, even in the worst rut. But if love has lost its edge, it needs sharpening.

After observing your relationships, ask God to show you which ones need your attention. Now be sure to listen to the next impression you get. And no fair pretending you didn't hear if the relationship God mentions is one you wish you had never started in the first place. "No, God, not that one," I can hear you moan. Okay, so praying to God about creative love is a little like playing Russian roulette; you don't know which chamber the bullet's in. I never said this love stuff was easy. Or even always fun.

Oh—and you can't cop out by claiming you're not a creative person. Everyone is creative; we simply have to learn how to access our creativity. One way to do this is to start varying your routine. Begin thinking outside of your box, whether that means what you "create" for dinner every night or the way you pray during your devotional time. Once you start acting more creatively, you'll be surprised at how many more creative ideas you'll discover, and they come right up from somewhere inside of YOU.

The third and last step, then, is taking action. Any kind of action. It doesn't matter so much what you do as long as you do something. No ideas? Read magazines. Get on the Internet. Talk to people. Ideas for creative love are everywhere—if you're looking for them. I was fresh out of ideas once for a close friend's birthday, and then I found out that she'd never been to San Francisco. At age fifty-two, she'd never ridden a trolley car! So we boarded a plane in Seattle and flew to San Francisco for lunch, then flew back in the evening. What a blast!

How about gathering a bunch of photos of you and an old friend over the years, putting them together in an album with captions for each photo, and presenting it to your friend—for a birthday or for no particular reason at all? One time I compiled all of the friendship songs I could find on one tape and gave it to a friend to let her know how much she meant to me: "The Wind Beneath My Wings," "That's What Friends Are For," "With a Little Help from My Friends"...

Creative love can rejuvenate relationships that have become dull over time. Creative love can cause close friends to become even closer. And creative love can draw people to you simply because while they never know what to expect, they know you're a person who is always engaged in thinking up new ways to love. That kind of person is one others want to be around.

Ask Yourself

With whom have I fallen into a rut in the way that I love?

How can I love more creatively today?

How can I make creative love an ongoing endeavor?

To Do

Set aside ten minutes to think about how well you're loving the people in your life. Then choose one person to love creatively today. You might want to encourage someone verbally, pointing out something you never have before. You might want to finally sign up for that volunteer program, something you've been putting off. You might choose to creatively love an enemy in some way, as my girls did. Whatever you decide, let it be something you've never done before.

Chapter Six

the nuances
of love

"Here today—gone tomorrow."

"Out of sight, out of mind."

"He loves me—he loves me not."

All of these sayings, programmed into our minds since childhood, speak of love's capriciousness. But love, real love, God's kind of love, is not capricious. God told the prophet Jeremiah to write these words in a book for future generations: "I have loved you with an everlasting love" (31:3). Here today—gone tomorrow? Not exactly.

I suspect the origin of these sayings lies in the nature of relationships, which are forever changing. As a result, the appearance and expression of our love can change from day to day.

In my church there was a certain very misunderstood woman I'll call Linda. She was in constant "trouble" with some of the other women because she would move in and out of their lives according to the needs she sensed at the moment. When someone had an operation, she was right there bringing a casserole or offering emotional support and prayer. Then, when she would hear of a couple going through a divorce, she was there with a nonjudgmental ear to listen. As a leader in the church, she was constantly grooming new leaders, each of whom she would be close to until it was time to groom others.

Linda was accused of being capricious in her love, disloyal, fickle in her friendships, all while she was going about "doing good." True, when Linda focused her attention on someone new—appropriately, given her calling and her position of leadership in the church—the person who had earlier been the center of her attention often felt hurt and left out. But the hurt feelings occurred not because Linda's love was capricious or because she had stopped loving that person; they occurred because the person had grown attached to Linda—perhaps in an unhealthy way—and couldn't understand why she was no longer as available as she once had been.

When we give love to others, we can do so knowing that if others place expectations on us or start making demands, it is their problem to work out. Love is to be given freely, no strings attached. When it is our turn to receive love, we can also do so freely, grateful that someone was listening to God in making himself available to meet our need. And then we can let go when the need is past.

My children have taught me a lot about love—its seeming capriciousness, its absolute constancy.

"Mom, I love you—you're the best mom in the whole world." But soon after my nine-year-old son said those words, I did something to make him angry, and he was closed off from me for two long years. Did he not love me during that time?

"Mommy, Mommy!" My two-year-old daughter runs to me when I pick her up from Sunday school and gives me a big hug and a kiss. But then the very next hour at home, she's screaming at me from her high chair and refusing to eat her broccoli.

My fourteen-year-old daughter brings me a rose she bought on the way home from school. Then that evening, late, I go into her room to check on her before I go to bed, and she's gone. Snuck out.

And am I any different? One day I buy my daughter a guitar, and the next I take it away from her because she hasn't done her homework. She might perceive my way of disciplining her as a very unloving thing to do.

When we yell and cry and close off, when we refuse to eat our broccoli, or when we sneak out in the middle of the night, is it a sign that we don't love someone?

Love doesn't always look like love. We can't put ourselves under the pressure to love according to another's idea of what love looks like. Only you and God know just how real and pure your love is. We are all responsible for ourselves and how we allow God to love through us. Our gifts are all different, and therein lies the beauty of love's nuances.

Human relationships are indeed capricious. And so, in a bigger sense, what we want to concern ourselves with is how to be God's constant expression of love in a world that may or may not perceive our actions as loving or that may even judge us for the way we love.

It can be confusing. You're reading this book. You're making a commitment to love your world. You're excited about the possibilities...and then a friend betrays you. Your child rebels. A coworker tells you off. Now what?

You keep loving. But what will your love look like in the midst of these new circumstances? Will it look like love if you back off from the other person for a while? If you stand up for yourself? If you set some boundaries?

Certain events, people, situations, and tragedies seem designed to throw us off center, to undo us, to challenge our commitment. These things will always be there, as long as we live in this world. But our circumstances are not the issue—the issue is that we continue to love in the midst of them even if our actions or behavior may be perceived as less than loving.

How can we, for example, remain true to ourselves and our commitment to love in the middle of a friend's betrayal? Regardless of how our actions are perceived as we process our feelings during the betrayal, we work through the emotional issues so that we come to a place of forgiveness and compassion, knowing that we ourselves are capable of betrayal.

Remember—both Judas and Peter betrayed Jesus. Why do we find it nearly impossible to comprehend Judas's betrayal, yet we can so easily forgive the bumbling fisherman?

Jesus loved them both the same. Their actions after their betrayals, of course, differed greatly, making it easier for Jesus to express his love and forgiveness to one more than to the other.

I believe God loves me. That is really the only reason I have the desire, the courage, the impetus to reach out and love others, whether or not my love is returned. It is the only reason you can reach out to love others.

The sacred question, I suppose, is, *What does it mean for me to love today, and what does it look like?*

The obvious answer is that it looks different on different days and in different people. But it always looks like God.

Ask Yourself

How do I gauge whether or not I'm loving? Or loving well?

Do I go by the signals others give me? By whether or not they can feel my love? Or do I trust the internal voice of the Holy Spirit inside of me?

How can I make love more of a constant in my life?

How can I love unconditionally no matter what is happening externally?

To Do

Know that God loves you. The more and deeper your assurance of God's love, the more deeply you'll be able to love others. Make it a priority to remind yourself today of how much God loves you. In order to do this, you may have to ignore the circumstances or the people who cast a shadow of doubt on your commitment. Trust your own heart. No matter how others perceive you or your actions, if *you* know that you are loving your world, that's all you need to know.

Chapter Seven

loving today
and tomorrow

By the time you get to be my age, you've loved a lot of people. Sometimes I wake up in the morning and I think: Out of all the people I owe e-mail and letters to, out of all the people I want and some I *need* to call, out of all the people I *should* make contact with, out of all the people I *will* make contact with today, on whom should I focus? Because loving my world is such an ever-present choice for me, it's never far from my thoughts. Sometimes it drives my days, sometimes I forget about it, but I always come back to it—because I want it to drive not just my days, but my life. I believe this is one reason we came to the planet—to love. Therefore, it's important that we get—and stay—in touch with how love is supposed to be worked out in our lives from day to day.

I look at my to-do list and I think, *I want to call Merilee* (my older daughter). *I haven't talked to her in a week. I wonder how she's doing.* But then the phone rings, and it's my friend with a problem.

I listen. I get off the phone and go to call Merilee, but she's not home. So I sit down to write a letter to one of the men I visit in prison. But then I remember I've owed another friend an e-mail a lot longer than I've owed the inmate a letter. And so the day goes. As does my life.

Loving our world is a series of choices, a constant centering of ourselves so that we know what God's "good, pleasing and perfect will" is (Romans 12:2). Whom does he want me to love today? How can I order my day around conscious acts of loving, and how can I know best on whom to focus today?

Loving others has a definite rhythm that we can be tuned in to. People in our lives come and go. We need to let them, no matter how much we might want to control them. Wouldn't it be wonderful if we could move more consciously with the ebb and flow? I believe God wants us to.

Do you think Jesus just walked the earth aimlessly, without any direction or destination? Given that he is God and is all-knowing, that would be impossible. Yet he was completely open to his days being disrupted—because he lived every minute of every day in touch with the Father's good, pleasing, and perfect will. How he spent his hours and days was determined not by everyone's urgent needs but by the Father's higher purpose.

We see it happening all the time in the Bible. When Lazarus was ill and his sisters requested Jesus to come heal him, Jesus was headed somewhere else. Interestingly, John tells us that "Jesus loved Martha and her sister and Lazarus. Yet when he heard that Lazarus was sick, he stayed where he was two more days" (John 11:5-6). Lazarus was not dead at this point, only sick, but Jesus didn't rush off to be with him just because those he loved thought he *should*. Ever rushed to do anything because someone else thought you *should?* Some of us order our days around what others expect of us. No, Jesus knew what he was supposed to be about every day, and he only let things "interfere" when he knew they were supposed to. His not going to be with Lazarus immediately didn't have a thing to do with his love for Lazarus or Lazarus's sisters.

Neither did Jesus feel obligated to explain to everyone why he was doing what he was doing. Don't you hate that? I always want to know why people do what they do: why they show up late for meetings, why they choose being with someone other than me, whether they have a good reason for not returning my phone call the same day I made it and what that reason could possibly be. But Jesus just kept doing what he was doing until he was good and ready to go to Bethany, and by that time Lazarus was dead. (Of course Jesus knew that; no wonder Mary and Martha had some difficulty with his "late" arrival.)

Could we ever live so consciously? That we would know, absolutely know, with whom we were supposed to be every single day? No matter what anyone else thinks we should be doing? I have hope we can know this, or if not *know*, at least come pretty close. We just have to stay in closer touch with God—and with ourselves so that we can hear God's voice. One thing about Jesus— he was always listening to his Father.

If it's true that loving our world has a rhythm, then how can we best tune in to the Father's good, pleasing, and perfect will and stay tuned in? First of all, we can trust our hearts. I used to think that being a Christian meant I couldn't ever do what I wanted to do because, since there's nothing good in me, if I *wanted* it, it must be bad. I now realize that this view doesn't hold much faith in God's ability to transform our hearts. I told God a long time ago that I wanted to live for him, and so would he please lead me? I'm trusting that he is answering that prayer by shaping the desires of my heart. And guess what? I *want* to love my world. This was a conscious decision I made after I decided I wanted to live for God. And if that's my desire, I can trust that God will lead my heart, will orchestrate my days, and will give me opportunities to love that I couldn't manipulate myself.

Assuming then that we *can* trust our heart, we need to begin to listen when our heart speaks, rather than repressing or ignoring it. There is a word for this process of learning to listen to our heart. That word is *intuition*, and we need to develop it.

Have you ever met someone and known the minute you met him or her that you wanted that person to be a part of your life for a very long time? You want the opportunity to *love* that person. Then there are others who, when you meet them, you wished you hadn't. Not only do you know you don't want them to be a part of your life for a very long time—you wish they would disappear that minute. That's intuition.

Once we've listened to our intuition, we get to choose whom we love. It sounds so methodical, so unspiritual, that we get to choose whom we love today and tomorrow. Many people don't even know they have choices. They don't even know what they *want*. It's a new concept to them to think that they could actually choose what they want to do on a given day—when it comes to loving or anything else. But when we can trust our hearts, meaning the way God moves through our hearts, we earn the freedom to make choices.

I heard about a woman recently, a Christian, who listened one day to God in her heart and chose to donate a kidney to a complete stranger. Here is someone who's definitely tuned in, who is answering the call to "love one another."

Today I'll love this person. Tomorrow it may be someone else. But I'll do it consciously, not because any one person lands in front of my face—although sometimes that may be the reason—but because I'm in touch with the Father, as Jesus was. Every day. Every moment. Always and forever. We serve a God who gives us unlimited choices and opportunities. And you don't have to let this overwhelm you. All you have to ask right now is "Who will I love today?"

Ask Yourself

Of all the people in my life, on whom do I *want* to focus this day?

Who needs God's touch today, and how can I best be the messenger for that touch?

How can I most lovingly deal with those who are clamoring for my attention but not getting it today?

To Do

Just for today, let love drive everything you do: whom you meet with, to whom you talk on the phone, with whom you spend time. Consciously guide your conversations so that each person who goes away from you feels loved. This is God's will for you today—and every day.

Chapter Eight

at home

"How can you talk like that to your sister?" I looked up at my six-foot-tall son. "I can't believe that if you talked like that to your friends, you'd have any friends left."

"Well, of course." He just grinned at me. "I don't talk like that to my friends. Well, there is this geek, Jed, that we sometimes..."

But I wasn't listening. What I'd heard already confirmed my point. "You don't? You don't talk to your friends like that. So then why—"

"Cuz they wouldn't hang around to listen," he said, still grinning a little sheepishly. "You guys aren't going anywhere. You'll still be here tomorrow no matter what I do or say."

These words were spoken by a teenager. And teenagers are often more honest—with themselves and with others—than adults are. We learn to hide our real feelings, our true motives, our honest thoughts. But my son voiced the truth that resides in our hearts even though we may never admit it: We can get away with treating our family members or those we live with poorly because we think they're stuck with us.

Home—it's supposed to be a haven, a harbor, a safe place where we can be ourselves and be accepted for how those selves are expressed. So how is it that in many homes, it's the exact opposite? The better we know people, the sloppier we get in the way we treat them.

There was a time in our family when one of my daughters was out of control. Every day would bring any number of rude outbursts toward me or other family members, any number of calls from the school or neighbors who had encountered her, and any number of reactions on my part.

I remember the day I woke up praying, "God, I choose to forgive her for the twenty-five things she's going to do today." It was a prayer I woke up with for many weeks and months to come. It was the only way I knew to survive this difficult period and not lose the relationship. I struggled not to take her lashing out personally and not to give up in despair when I had to clean up the havoc she wreaked on those around her. In reflecting back on that time, I would have to say my actions were some of the most conscious loving I've ever done.

Why is loving those we live with so difficult, and why do we so often do such a lousy job of it? I can think of at least five reasons:

1. We think we deserve at least one place where we can let down and not have to show our "nice" face.

2. We don't always like the people we live with very much, and so we think, "Why try?"

3. We're tired and stressed out a lot of the time, and we just want to be left alone when we're at home, so if anyone gets in our face...

4. We don't express our feelings as they surface, so they
        build to the boiling point.
    5. We take the people we live with for granted—they
        have to love us.

Let's take those five reasons, break them down, and discover a
way to make our commitment to love a reality at home.

1. First of all, why do we think we deserve a place we can let
down? And what does it mean to "let down" anyway? Why does it
have to mean being rude, nasty, and cantankerous? Or even sullen?

The next time you want to "let down," try being vulnerable.
Honest. Real. Try saying, "You know, I just need some space right
now. How about if we talk later, say, in a couple of hours?" This is
what the Bible calls "speaking the truth in love" (Ephesians 4:15).
So much more effective than "Get outta my face."

2. God doesn't require us to *like* the people we live with—or
anyone else, for that matter. What's required is that we *love* them.
But how can we love someone we don't like?

I'm not sure how it works. I just know that when we ask him
to, God changes our hearts and helps us transcend any personal
grievances we have toward others. I haven't always liked my
employers. Or my neighbors. Or my friends. Or, at times, even my
kids. But I've committed to love my world. And I've never doubted
that I loved my kids. The others? I'm committed to work at it, to
keep loving no matter if I feel loved by them or if they're acting
lovable.

3. Why should the people we live with always see the worst of
who we are? We get up in the morning, put on our recently
pressed, cleanest clothes, and paste a smile on our face to greet the
world. But when Dad gets home, he strips down to a T-shirt and
baggy sweats and with a growl in his throat plops down in front of

the television with the remote, and Mom puts the baby into a playpen in the same room with Dad and disappears into some on-line chat room for the rest of the evening.

We have to find a way to stay "up" at home at least for some part of the day. That's part of what it means to be committed to love. We may need to take short breaks during the day to pace ourselves so that we can be present to our loved ones at the end of the day. We may need a debriefing time before we can relax, a time for sharing the joys and pain of the day. I think this may be what dinner together used to be, not a time for gulping down food, but a time to listen to one another share about the day.

4. We don't *have* to keep our feelings locked up inside of us all day every day. We *choose* to. We also don't *have* to keep spewing over with everyone we encounter like the proverbial pot boiling over. We *choose* to do that, too.

I remember one of the first times I became conscious of my anger toward a coworker. I could continue to be passive aggressive in taking out my anger on her, or I could share my feelings with her. I decided to own my anger and tell her how I felt. Not only did it save our working relationship, but I didn't have to boil over on my family when I got home in the evening.

5. It's simply not loving to treat our loved ones any old way we feel because we know they'll get over it, because they're family and they have to love us. Love isn't about us. It's about making a choice to reach outside of ourselves to express God's love to someone else.

One woman I know, whose elderly mother has moved in with her, makes sure she spends at least one hour of every evening with her mom, doing an activity she will enjoy, whether it's working a jigsaw puzzle or watching a television show. This is after a full day of work when often she just wants to be alone and take a warm bath. But she has made a commitment to love her mother, and she wants to make sure she does it every day.

I know of one husband and wife in their seventies who turn their phone off every evening at seven o'clock so they will not be interrupted by the outside world. They can focus on each other.

Oh, and if you're one of those rare folks who don't have any trouble loving the people you live with, save this chapter. You may need it when your sweet little darlings become teenagers. Or when you and your spouse are past the honeymoon stage. Or when your mother-in-law moves in.

Ask Yourself

How do I treat the people I live with? In what ways do I take them for granted? In what ways can I be more loving when I'm at home?

What can I do on a daily basis to go the extra mile, to fulfill my commitment to love not just my world, but the people with whom I live?

How can I surprise my loved one(s) today with an act of kindness?

To Do

Just for one day, choose not to complain about anything or nag or lecture anyone in your home. Listen to the tone you use with your loved ones. Choose to be honest about your feelings and to own them before sharing them. Imagine today is the last day on earth you get to spend with those you love the most. Act accordingly.

Chapter Nine

on the freeway

If we don't think about *how* to show love to the world, we probably *won't* show love to the world. Not that we'll be hateful; we'll simply miss out on opportunities to love because we won't see them.

You can learn a lot about how loving you are just by watching how others respond to you or approach you. Our behavior is often mirrored back to us. There is an elderly door-to-door Fuller Brush man in Portland, Oregon, for example, who has had quite an impact on his little corner of the world. Now, you know how excited we usually are to see solicitors approaching our door. Yet everyone on this man's route loves to see him coming. Why? He's kind, he goes out of his way through rain or snow for his customers, and he genuinely cares about the people on his route. When he became ill recently, his love was returned to him as his customers all rallied around him to help until he could once again do his route.

What happens when you walk down the street smiling at those you pass? I try to look strangers in the eyes and give them a smile.

Sometimes they'll meet my eyes, sometimes they won't, but when they do, they smile back. A smile goes a long way.

Paul called us "Christ's ambassadors." He defines the term by saying that "God [is] making his appeal through us" (2 Corinthians 5:20). Every time we go out into the world in any capacity, we are representatives of Christ. In real life, an ambassador is a high-ranking diplomat who represents one country to another. Often, he has a specific mission when he goes out. Likewise, we are on a mission—to love our world with all the love encompassed in the Holy Spirit as he inhabits our lives on a daily basis.

Have you ever noticed that when you act in loving ways, it inspires others to do the same? Do you walk past litter or stop to pick it up? Taking care of the environment is part of loving it. At the store, do you let others who have fewer purchases get in front of you in line? On the freeway, do you let the car with its turn signal blinking move into your lane? (Sometimes I deliberately don't turn my blinker on until I'm ready to move over because I know there are too many drivers out there who will speed up if they see I want to get in—I'm such a cynic.)

Who do you want to be on the freeway? There are really only two choices—a rude driver or a loving driver. Oh, there is one more choice—an unconscious driver, barely a step above the rude driver in the love department. The results are the same: Whether we drive selfishly or unconsciously, we miss the opportunities God strategically places in our paths.

When we wake up in the morning and think about the day ahead, what is our focus? What we plan to accomplish, usually—with our kids, at work, on our errands, in our conversation with our lunch partner. Determining to love those we encounter in our day is a decision we can get in the habit of making, even if it doesn't often come naturally.

You never know the effect your one small moment of love might have on another person. I was invited to teach in a conference in Hawaii recently, and I told the director on the phone, "You know, I just want to thank you for inviting me to teach. What an honor! And then for you to pay all my expenses to such a fabulous place—I'm just so grateful." I went on and on, and when I was done, she said, "It really means so much to hear that. Some of the big shots just seem to take us for granted. They complain about their room, the food, something, and I just wonder if they ever even think about the fact that they're getting their way paid to Hawaii, after all. So I'm glad to know when someone really appreciates it."

One of my mentors once said that before she goes into any situation with anyone, she says to herself, "I commit this situation to truth." I've made this my affirmation as well. I find that it keeps me conscious in my encounters with others; if I'm committed to truth, I'm committed to love. When I'm committed to truth, I'm consciously aware of approaching any person, any subject, any problem nonjudgmentally and respectfully, without preconceived ideas. When I'm committed to truth, I honor both myself and others as together we seek better ways of understanding and loving one another. This mind-set has really helped make me more conscious over the years of being my authentic self, no matter whom I'm with.

We need conscious reminders. How about a prayer, something like, "God, I choose to be your expression of love in this situation with this person." Create your own statement of commitment, one that sounds like you, or an affirmation: "I am God's ambassador of love today in this situation." You're it. If you forget, your affirmation will come back to haunt you. With God's help, you can begin to recognize the everyday opportunities you have to love your world—and you'll act accordingly.

No, loving our world isn't just another item to add to our daily to-do list. It's not something we do; it's who we are. Ambassadors. God's appeal to the world. We are here to express his love as we're living our lives. And loving the world truly does give us energy, rather than take it away. It's why we were created.

Ask Yourself
Whom do I plan to encounter today? How can I prepare myself to love that person or those persons?

How can I remember to actively love those I may not have anticipated encountering?

To Do
Write out a scripture or prayer of commitment that will remind you of your decision to love your world today, wherever you find yourself. Write it down and keep it with you at all times. Pull it out and look at it occasionally. Let the words penetrate your consciousness so you get in the habit of saying them to yourself before each and every encounter "out there."

Chapter Ten

loving in the
face of fear

"Hi there. This is Sandy Carson-Hutchinson. I'm calling on behalf of the reunion committee. It's been thirty years…"

She rambled on for a few more minutes, but I didn't hear anything else she said. My mouth suddenly felt unusually dry, and my heart started tumbling around in my chest. It was the middle of June already. I knew I'd graduated—*we'd* graduated—from high school thirty years before, of course, but I guess I'd thought all my old classmates had forgotten about a reunion. I'd wondered why we weren't having one, but oh well… I wouldn't have to worry about it, I'd told myself, relieved.

But now my stomach began to knot up. I wasn't thin enough. Not that I was obese or anything, but I'd gained a few pounds. I wasn't successful enough. I hadn't published enough books, and none had made it to the bestseller lists. Or any list at all. Worst of all, I wasn't married. They'd think I was a total geek. A loser, for sure.

I felt a headache coming on. One of those kinds that last a very long time—an entire summer even. And I had so been looking forward to this summer. Now it was ruined. I was filled with dread.

My panic lasted for about two days. Long days. Days of trying to think up excuses for why I couldn't make it to the reunion. That headache I mentioned—it was settling in for the summer, all right.

And then a moment of clarity. Finally. Some semblance of sanity in this irrational crazy space I'd begun to inhabit ever since I'd received a five-minute phone call from one little woman (and she was little—I remembered) on the planet. I suddenly thought, *Wait a minute. I have become totally self-absorbed. This is ridiculous. I will go to my reunion not because I have achieved anything at all and I want to show off, but because God, in his graciousness, is giving me one more opportunity to love my world. And I'm grateful.*

Scripture tells us in 1 John 4:18-21, "Perfect love drives out fear, because fear has to do with punishment. The one who fears is not made perfect in love. We love because he first loved us. If anyone says, 'I love God,' yet hates his brother, he is a liar.... Whoever loves God must also love his brother."

We can't know for sure what was in the mind of those who did the formatting of this passage, but if we close the gap between those two paragraphs, we connect the two biblical admonishments—one having to do with fear, one with hate. During my two days of panic, my thought processes had taken a subtle turn from fear of my former classmates' opinions to contempt for my former classmates.

My thoughts in the shower the first day: *Oh, Kelly and Joanne are probably a lot fatter than I am. They were overweight even in high school.*

My thoughts as I drove down the freeway: *Well, last I heard Joe and Danny were both driving garbage trucks.*

My thoughts as I ate lunch the second day: *Oh, and Debbie and Rick don't even have any kids to brag about. They never wanted any. That's pretty selfish.*

And on and on until I finally caught myself. I had been dismissing my old friends so that I would not have to face my own inadequacies, insecurities, and fears in the light of my upcoming reunion. To be honest, it wasn't so much that I was afraid they would laugh (well, maybe a little), ridicule, and/or judge me for any perceived lack of success, but that in their presence, I would compare myself, be found wanting, and then have to deal with the painful reality of who and what I wasn't at almost fifty—all of which I managed to avoid in my day-to-day life.

This was big! All because of a little ol' high school reunion. Yet I knew, without even talking to God about it, that my love for my former classmates and ultimately for myself would move me beyond my fear.

I was right. When I walked into my reunion that first night intent on loving, not only did I renew old friendships, but I decided to reach out to those outside of my little clique. I ended up making new friends that I'm now e-mailing and writing to. At any time during the three-day reunion when fear threatened to paralyze me, I would focus on the other people there, walk over to someone I didn't know, strike up a conversation with someone standing alone. And I always made sure to keep a smile on my face for those spouses who didn't know a soul there.

Try it. When you're afraid of a job interview, a confrontation with a spouse, child, or friend, making a speech—tell yourself that those you're so intimidated by and afraid of are just human beings like yourself, simply in need of love. They may never admit it, and they may not act like they're in need of anything. That doesn't mean a thing. Deep down we're all the same.

When we love another person, we're closer to fulfilling the will of God than when we're doing anything else. But when we're facing fear, who's thinking about the will of God? We're thinking about protecting ourselves at all costs until we can either escape or annihilate the source of our fear. Fear is such a powerful force, and only one weapon in our arsenal can combat it: love.

And to love in the face of fear takes courage. A number of years ago I read one sentence in Walter Anderson's book *The Greatest Risk of All* that has continued to inform my life up to the present. He wrote, "Courage is always and only one thing: It is acting *with* fear, not without it." He goes on to say that "to be brave, we must be afraid. Risk-taking is not easy—and the greatest risk of all is to try to know oneself, and to act on that knowledge."[1]

To know ourselves is to know when we're afraid. To act on that knowledge is to pick up the one weapon in our arsenal that will defeat fear. In spite of the pounding chest. In spite of the feelings of insecurity and inadequacy. In spite of the anxiety that we'll be exposed as impostors. Losers. Unsuccessful, underachieving, fat geeks. Or whatever.

In the face of that kind of fear, can I love my world? Can you? When's your high school reunion? Any feelings? (Oh no—another very real fear—that I'm the only one on the planet with such pathetic, completely irrational anxiety about class reunions…)

Ask Yourself
What am I afraid of, and how is my fear affecting my ability to love others?

How does it keep me from reaching out? From being myself? From allowing others the privilege of knowing me?

To Do
Identify at least one fear that is controlling your life in a way that prohibits you from loving. Choose to target that fear until it's overcome. Face it. Overpower it. Conquer it. Remember that perfect love drives out fear. Your commitment to love others will ultimately take care of any and all fear connected to relating to them.

1. Walter Anderson, *The Greatest Risk of All* (Boston: Houghton Mifflin, 1988), 215.

Chapter Eleven

loving through anger

Doesn't loving through anger seem like an oxymoron? How can we love and be angry at the same time? If love is a feeling, then how can love and anger coincide in the same moment, in the same relationship, in the same home? It can, because as we've already seen in previous chapters, love is not only a feeling but a commitment. And part of that commitment means battling and working through anything that might hinder the flow of love.

Anger tests our commitment to love, that's for sure. Today I have periodic bursts of anger, as I'm sure you do, but there was a time when anger drove my days and nights—my life. I was angry at my ex-husband for "ruining my life." I was angry at "the church" for telling me who I should be in that marriage. I was even angry at God for allowing me to be in an abusive marriage, even though I was the one who had chosen my husband. I was angry about a lot of things.

My anger caused me to realize that I was falling far short of loving my world. I remember one day in particular when this was brought home to me. A friend and I were driving down the freeway. I was once again venting all my hurt about my divorce, my pain, my life, etc.

"You know, I can't keep being your dumping ground," she interrupted.

"Huh? Dumping ground? What are you talking about?" How rude. Was she saying I was throwing garbage at her? What was she saying?

"I believe we all need to vent from time to time, but this is going on and on and on. You have to move past it, don't you think?"

I was quiet, pouting.

"How can you love your world when you're mad at everyone in it?"

Loving my world was a concept I was just beginning to consider and had been talking about with her. When she said that, I was tempted to give up. Obviously, I couldn't be angry and love my world.

"I guess I can't," I said flippantly. "Oh well…"

I'd opt for being angry. I didn't think I had a choice, after all.

"So what are you going to do?"

"Do? About?"

"Being angry. Are you going to hang on to it or work through it so you can love your world?"

I couldn't remember having asked my friend for her opinion on any of this. But it started me thinking. Was it truly either/or? I had to give up one to possess the other?

If and when we decide we want to grow, we can use everything that life brings us to facilitate our learning. And anger, I'm discovering, is a wonderful motivator for anyone who wants to grow. The instant it shows up we want to take action of some kind—and the action we want to take is often less than loving. We have visions of...well...*hurting* people. Anger, in other words, can reveal our true nature at its worst. If we're committed to love, once we see our murderous intentions and it becomes clear that loving our world has taken a backseat to our baser instincts, we can't help but turn to God for help. We work through our anger so we can get back to love.

I make it sound so simple, don't I? It's not. Anger is a complex emotion, and while I don't pretend to be a therapist, I know anger has many layers that we sometimes have to dig through to find our way back to love.

Basically, we have to:

1. get validation for our anger so that we can fully express it
2. honestly evaluate whether we're blaming someone else for the situation causing our anger and if so, take personal responsibility
3. grieve the feeling underneath our anger (usually sadness and/or fear)
4. let go of our anger by forgiving whoever we're mad at and asking God to heal us

If we are able to move consciously through this process, we can get back to love. Let's look at each of these steps a little more closely.

1. How do we get validation? By expressing our anger to an objective party, someone who will let us be mad without telling us we *shouldn't* be or that feeling angry is a sin. Anger is a big threat to those who are uncomfortable with conflict, so if we want to get to

the bottom of it and be our authentic selves in the middle of it, we have to be careful to whom we express our anger.

2. How do we move past blaming if we perceive that others have played a part in hurting us? We can see that our anger is just that—*ours*. Others can abuse, use, harass, violate, torment us, but they can't *make* us feel anger. We choose that emotion because we're attached to something we're afraid of losing. My anger in the above scenario was complex, but it mostly had to do with my fear that I'd given up so much of my true self to that marriage, I was afraid I'd never find myself again—that I was forever screwed up. My anger with God had to do with my attachment to who I thought he was as Protector; when I faced the reality of the kind of man I'd married, I found myself questioning God's protection.

3. How do we get to the grief? We can ask ourselves what we're afraid of, what's making us sad. What do we wish were different in this situation? If we feel so inclined, we need to let the tears come. We have something to cry about, or we wouldn't be angry in the first place.

4. How do we let the anger go? We choose to forgive, or at least to start the process of forgiveness, and open ourselves up to God's healing in the area where we're hurting.

These four steps do not necessarily take place overnight. They may take days, weeks, months, even years. God doesn't push us, but when we're going over and over and over the hurt without moving through the anger, we know we're stuck on one of the steps.

At the end of the fourth step, if we're committed, we can once again get back to loving our world. This was true for me. When I'd wrestled through the core of a lot of my anger and done the forgiveness work, I lost that edge of bitterness that seemed to show up in my relationships and in too many conversations with others. I stopped being so critical of those who, through no fault of their own, were unwanted reminders of the source of my anger. I became more gentle and compassionate and long-suffering in my dealings with others who were in the middle of anger, because I only had to take a brief look back to see how many years it took me to work through my own.

It's unrealistic to think we're not supposed to experience anger, or having successfully worked through it once that we will never experience it again. Anger is normal. How we choose to move through it is the issue. A commitment to love our world will hopefully also keep alive a commitment to keep anger moving. Daily— because that's sometimes how often it surfaces.

Ask Yourself

Can I admit that I'm angry today at anyone in my life? Where am I in the process? On which step?

Am I stuck in anger? How can I get unstuck?

What do I have to do to get back to love?

To Do

Explore the anger in your heart. Feel comfortable with its presence without trying to change it into something else. If you can get someone to help you validate it, do so. If not, validate it yourself. If you're blaming, acknowledge that. When ready, proceed to grief, then to letting go of the anger. Welcome love back.

Chapter Twelve

when the feeling is gone

When we wake up each morning, all that God expects from us all day until we climb back into bed at night is that we love—him, others, and ourselves. How hard can that be? Not so hard—until something disappointing, disillusioning, or maddening happens. Then the people we loved yesterday don't seem so lovable anymore, and we put love on hold for a while. Oh, we might still hang around those disappointing, disillusioning, or maddening people, but our heart is no longer in it. We're down the road, on to better people who will appreciate us. Doesn't the Bible even say not to "throw your pearls to pigs" (Matthew 7:6)? Isn't that what we're doing when we're offering our love to those who can't or won't receive it? If we're honest, this is often how we justify no longer loving those we no longer *feel* like loving.

You know, we can find a scripture to support anything we're doing. Or not doing. And I suppose, if we're going to use a certain scripture to support a decision not to love, then we have the responsibility to ask the hard questions. The first obvious one to me would be: Who are we to decide exactly who is and who is not a "pig"?

The answer isn't that simple.

When a teacher commits to teach in an inner-city school, for example, she may start out with high hopes and a very real feeling of love for her students. Over time, after months, even years of too many abusive confrontations with some of her students, her enthusiasm and consequently her feelings of love start to diminish. But she chooses to stay because she knows she's doing some good in her students' lives and she knows the system needs her. She's committed in spite of how she feels.

I've heard of all kinds of folks who stay in abusive corporations, industries, systems, and even religious organizations once they have fallen out of love with their ideal—their fantasy of who and what various authority figures claimed to be. They stay because of their loyalty to "the little people," or to what they consider to be God's calling on their lives, or because they're just not quitters. They're committed, regardless of how they feel toward those within the system.

God has a plan for who and what we become in each situation, and we must make sure we're listening for his daily instructions on how to love—especially in those cases where we feel like bailing more than we feel like hanging in there and loving. But whether we understand his plan or not (as if we could ever hope to know how the Almighty's mind works), we can count on learning and growing—if we're committed to love.

That's the key. If you've made the commitment to love your

world, deeply and from your heart, every minute of every day, you've said a big, fat yes to God. You're open now for assignments. But being open to an assignment and completing an assignment are two very different things. Yes, I do believe our assignments have expiration dates, maybe temporary, maybe permanent. But just because we lose the feeling of love doesn't necessarily signify the end of an assignment to love. If the feelings are gone, yet down deep we know it's not time to leave someone's life, how do we make it day to day? How do we keep ourselves motivated? How can we better cooperate with God in loving a person or persons when, for whatever reason, the warm, fuzzy feelings have disappeared?

First, try to understand why you have lost your loving feelings. What happened? Did someone hurt you? Do you believe it was intentional? Is it possible for you to communicate your hurt feelings to the individual or individuals who hurt you? Oftentimes, people don't even know they've hurt us until we tell them. If you can communicate your hurt to the other person, you may find that your loving feelings will return.

The absence of feelings is always an indicator of something to which we need to pay attention. You may have numbed your feelings in an intimate relationship, for example, to protect yourself from intense feelings of rage that are just too scary to feel. You may have lost interest in an activity that required you to love a group of people because your heart truly has moved on. You may have once felt compassion when you walked past a homeless person but no longer do because you've seen one too many of them and the problem feels hopeless and overwhelming to you.

When did the feelings go and why?

Second, reevaluate the relationship and your commitment to

it. If we bail the minute we no longer feel like being involved, we often miss the opportunity God is providing for spiritual growth. The reasons behind our lack of feelings lead to deeper, more important questions that we need to consider before we take that first step away from active love. Questions like: Now why did I start doing this (e.g., enter into this relationship, start this volunteer work, join this organization) in the first place? Do I have realistic expectations of my role? What has changed since I first decided to engage in this area of loving my world?

Last, ask yourself what God expects from you now. There are no concrete rules for loving our world. Every journey is unique, and God calls each of us to travel it in our own unique way. I can think of at least one person from whom, when my heart turned cold, I walked away and never looked back. And I have the assurance, at least for now, that God is expecting nothing more from me in that relationship. Of course, because I've made a commitment to love my world and because as far as I know that individual still happens to be on the planet, if she ever pops up again, I'll have to reevaluate.

So what does God expect from us when it comes to loving our world? The prophet Micah gives us God's requirements: that we act justly, love mercy, and walk humbly with our God (6:8). As long as we keep our hearts open and we are committed to walk in active love whenever God requires it, we're following his will.

Ask Yourself

Have I "lost that loving feeling" toward someone or a group of people whom I'd previously committed to love? How did that happen?

As I honestly think about it, what is my intention toward that person or those people when it comes to active love?

Most important, what are God's expectations of me now?

To Do

Sometimes, when we experience an absence of feelings, if we act in loving ways, feelings follow our actions. Not always—they're not always supposed to. But sometimes. Think of an individual or individuals whom you know or even wonder if God is requiring you to love, yet for whom you have no loving feelings. Take a loving step toward that person. Do something.

Chapter Thirteen

when love
is silent

The little kid in me believes that those who claim to love me must do so in an animated way—lots of cards and letters, contacts, hugs, verbal affirmations, gifts and/or calls on my birthday, support during crises (of which I have many because I create them myself), etc. ad nauseam. I think that if I'm not hearing from someone, it means that person is not thinking about me and so, obviously, is not loving me. I'm definitely not a believer in the cliché, "Absence makes the heart grow fonder," but rather in, "Out of sight, out of mind."

But in the last few years, the grownup in me has learned better. I've accumulated a number of friends and business associates, and there's no way I can communicate with every one of them on a frequent, or even regular, basis. Does my lack of communication mean I no longer love these people? Of course not. I've taken many of them into my heart, and wherever I go, they will always be a part of me.

Even more importantly, I've learned that it's possible to consciously and deliberately—sometimes necessarily—love people from afar. To love them from a distance—not geographically, but emotionally. To love them silently.

I volunteer weekly in the men's reformatory near my home, and I've become friends with several of the men there. One of them, however, began to give me too much attention during my weekly visits, and I became concerned. I noticed that his letters were becoming more and more personal, then downright intimate. It was evident that he had imagined we had a romantic relationship which, in reality, wasn't even close to what our relationship was. Or would be. We were friends.

Soon after I realized how he was feeling, he was transferred to another prison. I decided the most loving thing I could do was to not answer his last letter. That was a year ago. I've thought about him many times, wondering how he's doing, whether or not he's happy (if one can ever really be happy in prison), how he's feeling about his life. We connected with each other in many ways, and I know he must have felt embarrassed to have laid out his heart so openly and not have the feelings returned. And he must have felt abandoned. I hate that—but I had to trust God and my gut on this one. I didn't believe we'd *never* have contact again; I just knew it couldn't be for a while. I never stopped loving him; I just loved him in silence. From afar.

What I sensed when I thought about how to love him "in actions and in truth" was that our love needed some purifying. My "action" for that moment in time was to step away from the relationship so that the "truth" could surface—the truth that our friendship could be one of loyalty and even commitment, but not romance. Stepping away in order to love is much different than stepping away because we're afraid or angry. Whenever you're feeling like you need to step away from someone, whether temporarily or permanently, make sure it's not out of fear or anger, but ultimately to love that person.

Friendship between men and women is tricky, I'm learning. But I'm committed to keep trying because I think it's part of loving others.

We can't always give love a voice. It doesn't always have a voice. And it isn't always possible to *express* our love, even if we want to. Love oftentimes wants, and needs, to be silent in its movement. For example, sometimes another person may set some boundaries with us, need some space, and whether or not we understand it, love means honoring that person's wishes. Or maybe if we're feeling insecure in a relationship, our once loving words become demands and efforts to control. The loving thing to do is to step away and work on our own issues and come back only when we've let go of our expectations and can once again love unconditionally.

The nature of love is that it needs to communicate itself—or so we have always believed. How, then, can love be simultaneously *present* and *silent*? A difficult thing to comprehend. If it's not bouncing around, we wonder if it's alive.

Yet sometimes in relationships we get to a place where every time we open our mouths, we make things worse. We think, *Oh, if we can just have one more conversation, I'm sure we can communicate. I'm sure we'll be able to hear each other.* We make the effort, but there's only more anger, more tears, more misunderstandings.

Rather than give up in despair, I'm learning to wait. Time and space often equal perspective. The problem is, for those of us who have abandonment issues (that would be me), time and space mean exactly that—abandonment. Yikes, that's the worst feeling in the world. Still, if we truly want to offer God's kind of love to the people he brings into our life, we must learn to wait, face the aloneness, and go where silent love wants to take us.

And where might that be?

1. Into a deeper level of prayer. When we're not enmeshed with others, whether kids, spouses, friends, or relatives, we can pray from a place of purity inside us. Our prayers begin to focus on the spiritual journey we're taking with the other person rather than on our often self-absorbed needs and wants in the relationship.

> *God, teach (name) and me to relate on a more compassionate level. Show us your purpose for this relationship. How do I need to grow to be a more loving person? How can I be more vulnerable, more open? How can I express my needs in a way that is not demanding? How can I become less egocentric and more Christ-centered? What do I need to detach from so that I can love more freely?*

Prayer like this can unclog our spiritual ears so that we can hear God's voice.

2. Into a deeper level of love. Space creates breathing room, allowing us to see, think, feel, hear, and sense everything more clearly. We can begin to see what the relationship with this person is all about. What our part is, what the other person's part is.

Instead of despairing that this may mean the end of a relationship, we can see that it may indeed be the end of something—something that needed to end—and the beginning of something else: a deeper level of commitment, a love that is purer, less self-centered, more compassionate.

3. Into a deeper level of action and truth. When we're praying and loving from afar, we can reevaluate without the emotion that often gets in the way up close. Space can give us a clear perspective of how much truth really exists in the relationship as it's been.

I know of one grown woman who saw the extent of her mother's emotional abuse only after she stepped away to love her silently. Loving her mother in the future will look different, as it will have to include more honest communication and less emotional involvement. Loving action in the future will have some boundaries attached to it.

Sometimes temporary silence leads to permanent silence. When that happens, we can only trust that we are where we're supposed to be. When we consciously step back to love silently, and in the long run, more honestly, we can trust that God is at work.

Ask Yourself

Is there anyone in my life for whom my love has become futile? Are my words only messing things up and making everything worse? Will stepping back from this person be more loving than stepping forward?

Is God asking me to love that person silently? If so, what is my responsibility as I wait? To pray, to attempt to recover feelings of love, to ponder how I might love this person more consciously in the future?

To Do

Consider your "difficult" relationships and whether loving silently may be the best option for right now. The time may be a year, a month, maybe even a day. Even one day away from a challenging time with your spouse or coworker can be a learning experience if you're willing to use that day to listen to God.

Chapter Fourteen

loving beyond

In work and relationships, we often do only what is expected of us because: (1) we don't want to be taken advantage of; (2) we want to be "healthy"; we don't want to enable anyone to use or abuse us; (3) we are self-absorbed, concerned mostly about our own schedule, our own agenda; or (4) we are lazy.

I could go on, but the point is, often in life we aim to meet only the minimum requirements, to just try to get by. Yet Jesus told his disciples, "If someone forces you to go one mile, go with him two miles" (Matthew 5:41). He gave this instruction in the context of how they were to love their enemies. Now simple logic tells me that if we are to go the second mile with our enemies, it's the least we can do with our loved ones.

In business, isn't it true that we frequent those places where we're treated the best? Oh, I know, some of us go for the cheapest. But I have been known to pay more for a product or service than I normally would if quality treatment is part of doing business with a company or individual.

When my car needs repairs, I think of a certain dealer because they always wash and vacuum my van. A small gesture, but it keeps me going back. The same with my dentist. I have moved all over the Seattle area, but I go far out of my way to my dentist because not only is she very qualified and gentle, she goes out of her way to accommodate my meager budget.

Well, that's business. What about work relationships, friendships, and familial relationships?

Last Valentine Day I decided to "go the extra mile" with my five kids and buy each of them a card with red suckers and red balloons tucked inside. None of them live with me, so we usually keep in touch by phone. Since we hardly ever write one another, my cards would come as a surprise.

I went to a card shop and selected a unique card for each "child" (they're all in their late teens through early twenties), grabbed some suckers and balloons, and headed back out to my car. I had an appointment, and I didn't want to be late.

The key was in the ignition when I remembered my ex-husband. I frowned. Why had he popped into my mind? (1) Because two of my kids lived with him. (2) Because my kids would receive cards from me on Valentine Day and he wouldn't. (3) Because he was a person with feelings, and I didn't want to hurt his feelings. And finally (4) he deserved a valentine, if for no other reason than that he'd given me five beautiful children.

It was that second-mile thing...a prompting that gets in your face when it's most inconvenient. I got back out of the car and returned to the store to hunt for one more Valentine card—no easy feat for an ex, I soon discovered. Eventually I found one I thought he'd like. I was now late for my appointment. But a few days later when he called to thank me, I heard a different tone in his voice. A softer tone. A less guarded tone. A kinder tone. And that tone has been there ever since.

I'm not always so good at this loving business. Like when I forget someone's birthday. Or yell at people in traffic—with or without my window down. And worst of all, when I withhold love from others because I want to self-protect or punish or look tough. But you know what? When we decide to love others, the opportunities don't slip by us the way they once did. God notices the nod of our hearts and begins to wake us up to opportunities to love. And to love more and better than we did before.

What would it mean for you to "love beyond," to go the second mile? To go out of your way for someone on any given day? To give more of yourself in a situation? To a certain person?

Consider the woman who forgave her son's murderer. Then, as if that wasn't enough, she began to write to him and visit him in prison, becoming his only supporter. I'd say she went not only the second mile, but the third and fourth.

A recent news report showed neighborhood families working tirelessly all night, placing bags of sand around one family's property to keep it from flooding.

And what about the attorney who works for nothing because he knows his client is truly innocent but has no money to hire him?

Magnanimous folks? No, folks just like you and me who, when faced with an opportunity, chose to love beyond what anyone expected of them.

Okay, so what does it mean for you to love your kids beyond what you're doing now on a daily basis? Your spouse? Your friends? Your coworkers? Your enemies?

I can hear you asking: "But won't I be taken advantage of? Won't I be used? I've spent too much of my life already taking care of everyone else…" Thanks to the idea of codependency that came out of the addiction recovery movement, we're sometimes overly concerned these days about doing too much. But I believe one of the reasons many people have so little energy is because they're not doing enough of the things that matter.

Loving beyond what's expected of you—I can almost guarantee it—will give you energy, not take it away. Here are a few ideas to get you started.

- Your child wants a ride to a friend's? Leave early so you can stop at Baskin-Robbins for an ice cream cone.

- Someone at work sends you an e-mail. Answer it, then add a sentence or two of encouragement—praise for a job well done, a compliment on how well he or she handled an awkward situation in the office, a "cheer up" after bad news.

- You find out your friend has cancer? Don't just send a card or e-mail. Offer to go with her to chemotherapy and arrange for people to bring her meals when she is sick in bed. Go beyond what is expected. Every day.

Going the extra mile takes only a moment out of our lives, yet the effects can be far-reaching. To love beyond is to cultivate an attitude of generosity toward the people God brings into our lives.

Ask Yourself

Who in my life right now can I love beyond what's expected of me? How can I go the second mile in my efforts to love this person— practically? Today?

Who can I take completely by surprise because this person expects nothing at all from me? Today, how can I love this person beyond my normal routine?

To Do

Make a list of words and phrases that will remind you to love beyond. Words like: *besides, in addition to, more, further, over and above, the second mile, over the top...* Now make signs to post at different places in your home, your office, your car to remind you to go beyond where you've gone before in loving others. Choose one person on whom to focus today.

Chapter Fifteen

refueling

When I first committed to loving my world, the idea was new and exciting. The thought of reaching out to someone beyond my backyard intrigued me. It seemed novel. A great adventure. I was confident I could take it on.

But now there are times I'm not so sure. Loving the world can be exhausting. People who need love—and that includes every person on the planet—can drain you.

Don't you wish we could have watched Jesus in action—you know, been right there to watch how he did this stuff? My guess is that being the wise (not to mention perfect) man that he was, he knew how to pace himself. He didn't wait until he was sick to death of everybody bugging him, then run away from them screaming, "Leave me alone!" (That would be me. And sometimes that would probably be you.)

Yet Jesus was constantly "withdrawing" from the folks he loved.

"Jesus...withdrew again to a mountain by himself" (John 6:15).

"Jesus...went off to a solitary place, where he prayed" (Mark 1:35).

"Jesus...withdrew by boat privately to a solitary place" (Matthew 14:13).

I'd sure like to know where that solitary place was. For many years, the only solitary place I could find was the bathroom. If you have a teenager or two yourself, you know it's not solitary for long.

The point is, if we're feeling drained and burnt out by our commitment to love others, we need to step back and refuel. We need to take a second look. Ponder what we're doing. Ask why we're doing what we're doing. Reflect. Consider whether our methods are working or whether we should change our strategy.

Maybe you're trying to love a difficult person, and this person is not responding the way you think he or she should. Or maybe you started loving someone in hopes that your love would bring about a change of some kind. Not a good reason to love, but we all do it. Maybe you're now realizing the person may never change. Maybe you've lost your focus and become unhealthily enmeshed with another person. Maybe you're just in a rut and wish you could think of more creative ways to love someone. Whatever the situation, what you need is to step back and reevaluate your motives, your desires for the relationship, and whether or not you still want to make loving this person or these persons a priority in the context of all the other areas of your life.

Jesus withdrew to a solitary place for different reasons. Sometimes it was to spend time with the Father. We can guess that they discussed profound subjects like the meaning of life—specifically Jesus'—on the planet, and his agenda for the next day or week.

Other times Jesus went to a solitary place because people wanted to kill him for some reason or other. Good reason to absent oneself from the premises! And I would wager a guess that sometimes Jesus went off to a solitary place to go fishing. To recoup. To catch his breath.

Life, with its many activities, with its people so in need of love, can consume us. We feel pushed and shoved to go faster, get more done, run here and there—clean this, call so-and-so, drive there, be at that meeting... The demands never end. Or maybe we've lost our focus, the reason we're loving in the first place. So many reasons to refuel.

As I've mentioned, one of the places I'm focusing my love these days is in a men's prison where I volunteer once a week.

I walk in and immediately have five or more men at my side—various bank robbers, drug addicts, murderers...

"Hey, Glo, how ya' doin'?"

"You're lookin' good tonight."

"I've been wanting to talk to you."

"Over here. C'mon, you've been ignoring me for weeks now."

And on and on. The testosterone is flowing in the room, and I'm the center of attention. All of a sudden I'm flirting too much and losing my focus. Nothing wrong with a "little" flirting, but I'm losing my center—the first indication that it may be time to refuel.

Sometimes I decide to stay away from the prison for a week or more to regain my focus, to center myself and remind myself that I'm up there for mainly one purpose—to share a bit of God's love. To bring a smile to a young inmate's face. To make a moment less lonely for an older inmate. To shatter, even momentarily, the isolation they feel day after boring day.

But I'm learning how to use Jesus' departing to a solitary place as a metaphor, and when I can't always literally and physically "depart," I go on an internal journey to a solitary place. If I feel tired or lose my focus, I'm learning to go inside of myself and pray, "God, remind me why I'm here. Make me a very real expression of your love. I choose to focus on *(name)* and let him know he has value, that he's not abandoned, that someone cares about him. Even if it's only for this one night and I never see him again [the inmates are often shipped out at a moment's notice, never to be heard from again], may your love through me have the kind of staying power that will comfort him long after this evening is over."

Withdrawing to a place of inner solitude works, and I'm back on track. I can't overestimate the value of these quick refueling moments in the middle of a crowded room or a busy day.

Our internal minijourneys to solitary places are important to help us maintain our focus in the short term. Dealing with those long-term assignments that drain our energy over months and years of loving is more difficult. We don't know how long Jesus' withdrawals lasted—hours, days, a week? Who knows? But just as he withdrew to renew his sense of purpose during those times, so must we move away from the crowd to ask ourselves some important questions. To contemplate our strategies. To evaluate whether our efforts are achieving results, or whether visible results are even something we're supposed to be looking for.

There is more than one way to "depart." You might want to take the phone off the hook for a certain amount of time each day, maybe when your kids are napping. You might need to get up in the middle of the night to spend time with the Father. When my children were small, a friend and I would trade off childcare for a few hours once a week. One time I rented a room at the Holiday Inn a mile from my home and hired a baby-sitter for a weekend.

I have varied my methods for achieving solitude over the years. Now that I live alone, of course it's much easier—if I remember to do it before I get tired and cranky. We can always find activities to fill our days; setting aside time to refuel will only happen if we see the importance of it and if we make it happen.

When we *know*, absolutely *know*, that God has called us to love—whether a certain individual, a group of individuals, the world—then it is our responsibility to honor that calling with a clear focus. To protect our calling from getting sidetracked by interesting detours that appeal to our egos, muddied by confusing emotional attractions, or weakened by a loss of physical energy. We need to depart regularly to a solitary place to recharge our spiritual battery.

If you're feeling burned out, consumed, or distracted in your commitment to love, stop. Take a breath. Step back. Go to a solitary place. It's the only way you'll be able to gather the energy you need to stay on the journey of loving your world.

We owe it to ourselves, to God, and to the recipients of our love.

Ask Yourself

Is there anyone in my life that I'm tired of loving? Is anyone draining me? Is this person my sacred work right now, or am I letting this person consume me in an unhealthy way?

Is it time to depart to a solitary place to refuel so that I can come back loving harder? Where can I go where no one can find me?

In the future how can I become more conscious of when I need to refuel *before* I'm totally drained?

To Do

Take a hard look at your calendar today, and whether you think you need it or not, schedule a time for solitude, for recharging, for refueling. Ask why you're doing what you're doing. Reflect. Consider whether your methods for dealing with life are working or whether you should change your strategies. The busier you are, the more often you need to depart and the longer you need to make the time away. Consider making this departure a regular thing—daily, weekly, and possibly an extended weekend every month.

Chapter Sixteen

choosing love again

"I'm done. I'm not doing that anymore."

"Huh? What?" My friend Sue looked up from her sandwich, seeming only mildly interested in my announcement. She was used to my making rash statements only to change my mind five minutes later when the situation changed, and with it my feelings.

"Loving people. No one cares, you know. I'm the only one who showed up at that volunteer meeting last night at the prison. Well, unless you want to count that old guy who couldn't hear. And that Mothers Against Violence meeting last week. All of five mothers were there—out of the entire community!"

"That's terrible." My friend nodded while munching on her ham and rye.

"I get tired of being the only one," I muttered.

"Become a cynic then," my friend suggested in a helpful tone.

"I am. That's what I already am. A cynic." I frowned, thinking.

Was that the only alternative? Cynics are kind of argumentative and negative. Archie Bunkerish. Who wants to be like that? Wasn't there anything in-between?

I'm always threatening to quit this loving business. Go on strike. Whatever. It gets so tricky sometimes. I even tell God this. "Okay, God, I quit. Loving my world has ceased to be a rewarding adventure and has become a pain in the—well, let's just say I'm not getting anything out of it at the moment."

But then I remember that I didn't make a commitment to consciously love others every day for my personal gratification or because there would be some kind of payoff down the road.

As we've seen, the world needs love, and you and I are the ones God chose for the job. Choosing to love has nothing to do with you or me making some kind of deal—if we give this amount of love, we'll get an equal amount returned to us. Sometimes that happens. Sometimes we receive more love back than we give. But that's a serendipity. There are no guarantees.

And so, when we tell God that we are willing to become his lovers in the world, we do so with no strings attached—to anyone or anything.

Yeah, right.

I wish I loved so nobly. Unfortunately, we sometimes do attach strings to our love, and when we pull them and people don't move or when we feel as if we're the only ones even making an attempt, we get hurt.

In my volunteer work at the men's prison, I try to stay focused, to visit with a giving spirit, to be like Jesus, dispensing love and goodwill to each and every person who crosses my path on that one evening each week. But every so often I get annoyed at the inmates. Like when I drive the fifty miles to see them and a few of them don't show up. Or when I bring a speaker, and the guys are less than attentive, whispering constantly to other inmates, not reaching out to my guest during the break, and squirming around in their chairs.

And so I stay home the next few weeks and pout. "I'll show them. They just don't get the pleasure of my company. They don't deserve blah, blah, blah…"

What? And just exactly when did I start expecting a bunch of felons to sit quietly and politely in their chairs like a group of altar boys? For even ten minutes, let alone two hours? And when did this giving, loving thing I've been doing become about their deserving my company rather than about what God is calling me to at this time in my life?

It's embarrassing, isn't it, when we see what's really in our hearts? Our egos keep getting in the way, and then our unconditional love so easily turns into very conditional love.

Yes, we get hurt when we love. Yes, we get our love thrown back in our faces. Yes, we're not always appreciated for our commitment to love. We can't and shouldn't deny the pain and the sometimes bitter feelings that surface at these times. God never requires us to ignore, refuse to acknowledge, or deny the difficult feelings that rise up on the journey of loving others. He simply requires that we depend on him to help us transcend them, to rise above them.

This doesn't happen easily. We need to take the time to process the feelings that cause us to question our commitment. If we don't, we will become resentful toward those we are committed to loving. In his letter to Timothy, Paul defined God's kind of love when he said it "comes from a pure heart and a good conscience and a sincere faith" (1 Timothy 1:5). How can these three things be applied practically to those times we've been hurt and are wondering if we can once again engage in loving others?

1. Loving with a pure heart. This verse isn't saying that we're expected to love perfectly. We're certainly to aspire to perfect love, and since we're made in God's image, I believe we can keep coming closer to it. But by its very nature, our humanness is an obstacle to our having pure motives 100 percent of the time.

For me, loving with a pure heart means that I acknowledge and surrender to God anything that would block my commitment to love: the resentment that builds up when someone I love is unresponsive, the discouragement that surfaces when I tire of being the only one who seems to care, the jealousy that springs up when someone I perceive as undeserving receives more and better opportunities to get ahead in some arena to which I aspire.

When I'm able to name my feelings and engage in an honest dialogue with God about what I feel and what I want to feel, I'm able to redirect my focus off my hurt and on to loving again.

2. Loving with a good conscience. The word *good* is sometimes a hard one to pin down, but in this context, I think I'm close when I say that "to love with a good conscience" means to love with no strings attached. Our conscience is that part of us that warns us when we're off track, when we're loving for reasons that are self-serving rather than other-centered. When I lose my focus concerning the men I visit in prison, I momentarily become more interested in whether they're behaving appropriately or whether I'm getting enough attention. I eventually wake up and see the strings attached to my love. My conscience prods me to let go of my demands and expectations, to love once again with the kind of love that is free of any self-serving motives.

3. Loving with a sincere faith. Could this be the kind of faith that simply believes the best of other people, believes they're doing the best they can, so we can give them a break?

Believing the best of other people doesn't mean letting others abuse us or treat us with less respect than we deserve as people created in God's image, but it does mean having compassion for those who hurt us. It does mean believing most people do not wake up each morning dreaming up new ways to torture us and make us miserable. And it means that when someone does hurt us, we won't feel compelled to retaliate or tear them down in some way—because we will realize that their actions arise out of their own deep hurts.

And so we can choose to love again. And hurt again. And love once more.

Ask Yourself

Who has recently hurt me? Am I on the verge of giving up on my commitment to love someone because of being hurt? If so, how has that affected my ability to reach out to that person?

Have I unconsciously closed off—to the world or to a particular person? What is one step I can take back toward "the world" or that individual to prove that I'm willing to engage myself once again as a lover?

To Do

To ensure that you're moving toward others rather than away from them, stay conscious of your feelings, especially those painful ones that surface in your interactions with others. Choose a partner, someone you trust, and commit to holding each other accountable for your commitment to love and love again. Ask each other on a regular basis, "What feelings did you have today? How did those feelings affect your commitment to love your world?" This simple act of accountability to another person will keep you conscious of your tendency to close off when hurt.

Chapter Seventeen

receiving love

I watched my good-looking neighbor help my roommate into the house with her groceries. I just stood there and scratched my head as he hauled in bag after bag while she batted her eyes at him and made a lame attempt at greeting her three children, whom I had looked after while she was grocery shopping.

What was the deal? I'd lived in this house for five years, I had *five* children, and my neighbor had never once offered to help me with my groceries. To be honest, since a huge bush bordered our properties, I'd never even met the man. But she moves in, and one week later he's over here being Mr. Helpful.

Not long after that, the clutch in my car went out, and after calling around, I found out what part I needed, and I fixed it myself. I was pretty proud of myself too—until my roommate's car broke down on the freeway and she immediately received at least five offers from guys in our church to fix it. These same men had known about my clutch, and not one had offered to help *me*. Well, now that I thought about it, maybe it had something to do with the way I'd told them about the problem.

"What am I doing this weekend? I'm fixing the clutch in my car," I'd said, a little boastfully. "It went out last week, and I've got the part, and someone told me how to put it in." I wasn't about to have anyone thinking I was some weak woman, some wuss who needed a man to help her—with anything. Now that I thought about it, my roommate didn't seem to mind at all if anyone thought she was a wuss; she had a look about her, a look that said—well, screamed actually—"Help me!"

What I didn't understand for a long time is that receiving love, letting others love us, is part of loving our world. If we carry around the attitude that we don't need anyone, that we are sufficient in ourselves, we rob others of the opportunity to love their world. I am a part of your world, and you are a part of mine. Loving one another suggests an exchange, a two-way street. I love you, you love me. Not—*I will graciously extend my love to you, and you can do the same—when I yank your chain. Which won't be often because, well, it's embarrassing. When I have a need I'll meet it myself, thank you. Stand by for an emergency. But I can take care of myself.*

Receiving love from our world is sometimes a lot harder than giving love to our world, I think. Why is that? Why is it so difficult for some of us to express a need to another person? For me, it's a combination of pride and the fear that once I express a need, no one will care enough to love me in that moment. I'll set myself up for rejection and the affirmation of this little thing in me that nags, "No one cares, no one's watching out for you, it's a dog-eat-dog world, yada, yada, yada…" When I'm in this frame of mind, I don't usually see that I'm not giving others the opportunity to love their world. I'm blind to that. I perceive this attitude as taking care of myself so that I don't set myself up for disappointment. But I'm growing in clarity, and I can more quickly than ever before see the fallacy of this way of thinking.

Now, I do know some people who too easily and too quickly let others take care of them. Haven't you known people like that— who just seem to enjoy sitting back and letting others take care of them? They get resentful when they have to do anything for themselves. They think God and the rest of the world *owe* them. That's not what I'm talking about here, and if you're one of those people, you have another whole set of problems to work on.

But until we see that receiving love is every bit as important as giving love, we will have an unbalanced perception of what it means to love our world. So how do we do it? How do we make ourselves available to receive love, thereby giving others the opportunity to love their world?

You can start by looking around you and assessing your needs. Sure, some of them you can meet yourself. But you lack resources to meet all of them. When my kids were small, a friend of mine, a math coach, used to come over once a week and tutor my son in math. I couldn't do that. Too many numbers in my head quickly turn to mush. This same friend built a fort in the backyard with another of my sons. Could I have done that? Well, I did put up a basketball hoop once, but building a fort was over my head, and I knew it. During my divorce, I was an emotional mess, and I needed lots of support. I was just learning about love then, and while it was one of the hardest things I'd ever done, sometimes I just needed to call a friend on the phone and cry.

What do you need help with? Is there anything keeping you from asking for it? If your problem is like mine and you sometimes think others don't care, you'll never know for sure until you get out there and find out, until you give others the opportunity to disprove your cynicism. The only reason I know today that some people do care and care deeply is because I've asked for love and received it. Not every time, but often enough to know that there is a community of those who are actively loving their world, just like you and I want to do.

Try to remember that receiving as well as giving is loving. The next time you're hurting or lacking in any area of your life, go ahead and risk asking for help. God has given gifts to all of his children, and it's up to us to enable one another to use those gifts to build his kingdom.

Ask Yourself

Is anyone trying to love me? Am I resisting because of pride or because I think others don't care? Explain.

On the other hand, do I too eagerly accept another's invitation to love me? Do I use people? Explain.

Which extreme would describe me, and how can I come to a balance?

To Do

The next time someone offers to meet one of your needs, consider whether this might be an opportunity to love your world by letting another person love you. If this is difficult for you, you may have to go as far as to actually confess a need to someone and ask for help. Or if you are too eager the next time someone wants to help, consider loving your world by turning down the offer and finding a way to meet the need yourself.

Chapter Eighteen

listening to love

I didn't like Catherine from the first moment I laid eyes on her. There was just something about her... But as followers of Christ, we've been taught that we are supposed to love everyone—no matter how we *really* feel.

So what are we supposed to do when we run into a Catherine, someone who annoys us? No, that's not completely honest. Someone who really irritates us? Still not quite honest. The truth is there are some folks we can't stand to be within ten feet of. And when we meet up with them, we want to ask God if he really meant it when he said, "Love one another.... By this all men will know that you are my disciples, if you love one another" (John 13:34-35).

No, I wasn't too great at loving when it came to Catherine. I'd run the other way anytime I saw her coming. Or hide under my desk. Avoiding her became inconvenient though—because, you see, Catherine was my boss. And so she tended to come around a lot. A lot more than I was comfortable with.

Why I didn't like Catherine is irrelevant. What's important is that I had a few things to learn about love from my relationship with her. I could run from Catherine. I could hide. But not if I wanted to grow in love. What could love teach me?

Listening to love means a number of things. But let's look first at what it doesn't mean. It doesn't mean denying our real feelings or pretending to love when we really don't. It doesn't mean being a martyr. Or a victim. Or a silent sufferer.

Listening to love means allowing difficult relationships to teach us some lessons, important ones like compassion, mercy, forgiveness, long-suffering. (You know, the stuff that works in us and makes us more like Jesus.)

I'm learning that listening to love means going beyond the surface of a negative reaction to someone. When I stop and think about why I'm responding negatively to a person, it's often because I see something in that person that I don't like in myself. What I hated in Catherine were the same things that I hated in myself. The things I couldn't seem to change. The stuff I hadn't resolved. And here she was—my mirror image presented to me five days a week every week for what turned out to be three very long years. God was giving me the opportunity to change—by showing me all of my unloving actions and reactions. I could grow—*if* I was willing to listen to love.

And I did grow. During those three years I learned some important lessons from watching Catherine: (1) that I would sometimes try to get my needs met by bullying others; (2) that since I perceived vulnerability as a character weakness, I had to be strong in all of my interactions with others; (3) that fear was too often making me hostile toward others, that I was holding a me-against-them attitude, making it impossible for me to love them.

If our hearts are open, love always has something to teach us. That's the one requirement—an open heart.

My friend Pam is a beautiful example of this. Ready to leave a women's group because of an obnoxious member, she told me one day, "I want to leave so badly. I can't even stand to be in the same room with Diane. But I have to know what my reaction to her is all about, why she brings out this hostility in me. I can't leave until I've learned what it is in me that Diane touches, that part of me I need to accept unconditionally." I was proud of her for even seeing that something bigger was going on than her own personal feelings for Diane. Usually, that's the case.

As uncomfortable as it is, like Pam we must be ruthlessly honest with ourselves. We can hear love's voice only when we refuse to avoid, deny, and/or defend our real feelings.

Avoidance: *Here comes Catherine. Wonder what she wants. Think it's time for a rest room break.*

Denial: *Catherine? Sure, I like Catherine. I have no problem with her. She's my sister in Christ, of course I love her...*

Defensiveness: *I have a good reason not to like Catherine. Plenty of good reasons, actually. Look at the way she treats us, how bossy she is, always telling us what to do, giving us too much work...*

When we're in any of these modes, we're not listening. To listen means to step back, be quiet, and open up. Then we can commit to telling the truth about how we really feel. Unfortunately, telling the truth is often where we get hung up. We fear that if we tell the truth, God will condemn us. So we lie—to ourselves and to God. But God wants us to tell the truth. Not so he can condemn us, but so that he can help us see our hearts for what they are and help us change and grow.

And growth can take place only if we're willing to listen. Avoiding, denying, and defending take a lot of focus, time, and energy. We can't hear love when we're putting our energy elsewhere.

I've often thought about what the writer of Proverbs 27 meant when he wrote: "As iron sharpens iron, so one man sharpens another" (v. 17). I believe that "iron sharpening iron" is assisting others in their growth in character.

I got really sharp working with Catherine. I learned that listening to love goes beyond heart transformation. It's also about how we *act* in the world *with* that changed heart. Regardless of whether or not I liked Catherine, I knew I needed to respect her as my boss. That's what I prayed God would do in my heart—give me respect for her. I began to see that Catherine's refusal to show any vulnerability didn't mean she was any less human than I was. I wanted to honor her spiritual journey the best I could, even though it wasn't the way I would choose to pursue my own journey.

The other day I heard a woman say that she was choosing to perceive her abusive ex-husband as her teacher, that he had taught her what she would never again tolerate from another human being. Catherine was my teacher in the same way; she was abusive to her employees, and I knew that after I left this job I would never again put myself under the authority of an abusive boss.

It almost happened again this year, seven years after Catherine. But the first moment my new boss raised her voice at me, I knew I wouldn't be staying. I quit the next day. No job, no relationship is worth allowing others to abuse us. Listening to love also means knowing when to leave.

When we're listening to love, we begin to understand that we are all one another's teachers. We sometimes miss that in our hurry to run or hide under our desks when we see certain people approaching.

You know—that lady down the block who talks so much. Or that kid who keeps asking the same dumb questions over and over.

That coworker who keeps criticizing you behind your back. These people can be our teachers, and if we truly want to grow to be more like Jesus, we have to begin to honor their roles in our lives. They teach us to look at those dark sides of our personalities from which we try to distance ourselves, those parts we have refused to integrate because they are so distasteful to us. These people teach us that even those unlovable parts of us are loved by God—unconditionally. From them, we learn to be more gentle with ourselves, more tolerant, more long-suffering. If we can stand still for a moment and become open instead of irritated, we can quietly ask: "What do you have to teach me?"

I remember such a moment. It happened after church one day. A friend and I were standing out on the sidewalk, engaged in an intense, serious, profound conversation—so intense, serious, and profound that I was crying, which I hardly ever do in public. We barely noticed the slightly disheveled, mentally impaired individual walking by until he approached us with a big, childlike smile on his face.

"Excuse me," he said.

Not now, I groaned inwardly. I sighed and turned toward him. I seldom gave money to homeless people, but maybe a quarter would send him quickly on his way. This was really annoying.

"I think you need a hug," he said and grabbed both of us around the neck.

Too shocked to react, I let him hug us, and then I found myself easing into the hug.

He backed off then, as abruptly as he'd approached. "You know," he said, throwing his hands up in the air, "God just loves us all." And he bounded down the sidewalk and around the corner.

I cried harder. In public. God had just sent us a messenger. And my role was to listen.

Ask Yourself

What is love teaching me today through those around me? The ones I have honestly thought had nothing much to say?

How can I stop and listen to love? Can I set aside judgments, preconceived notions, and misconceptions in order to be open to love's teachers?

To Do

Look around you. Who are your teachers? Just for today, put aside any notion of superiority and whether your learning opportunity is with a Catherine or a homeless person, choose to listen with your whole heart.

Chapter Nineteen

loving in and through the darkness

What does darkness look like to you? Loneliness? An inability to pay the bills? Out-of-control kids? Being misunderstood? What? Darkness means something different to every person. To one it might mean depression. To another, divorce or the death of a loved one. To yet another, the presence of evil.

Darkness doesn't play favorites. Whether the darkness is yours or another person's, it comes into all of our lives at one time or another. I've had many dark times in my life, some of them spawned in my own head, some of them taken on as I've suffered with others through their darkness. These times used to mean closing up shop and feeling sorry for myself. For a few years, it meant alcohol consumption by the gallon—or so it seemed. My life seemed shrouded in darkness, and coping was all I could focus on.

Is it possible to love our world during those times when we can't even see because of the blackness all around us? I believe it is. I've learned that darkness doesn't necessarily require checking out. We have more control over the darkness than I had initially thought. I'm learning to embrace darkness, even to keep love alive in the darkness. Darkness brings with it one more opportunity to watch God work in and through us.

I have an alcoholic friend in my life, someone I love very much. When this alcoholic was living with me, I tried to help him. I drove him around while he looked for a job, made sure he got to his job, confronted him when he came home drunk, and refused to give him money for alcohol. I thought I was doing all the right things. Then one day I couldn't watch the results of his drinking anymore, and so I moved—leaving him behind. Oh, I'd given him plenty of warning. I felt good about my decision. You never want to "enable" an alcoholic, after all.

We do the best we can in the middle of the darkness. But afterward, when giving ourselves a moment to reflect, sometimes we wonder, *Did I really do the loving thing?* Is it always right to do an intervention? Are we always enabling when we take care of an alcoholic? Who knows? And does it make a crucial difference in every situation? This person simply feels lost to me. What is my role in his life? Sometimes I want to gather him up and tell him it's going to be okay, that I'll always take care of him, no matter if he drinks the rest of his life. Other times I wonder if I'm strong enough to be in his life on a daily basis if he continues to drink. He's not ready to help himself, I know that.

The question then, always, is, What is love in this situation? It's dark, and there is no light on the horizon. These are the times we wrestle with everything we've ever been taught about God, love, the "rules." How do I love this person? Or the homeless man on the corner? Is it love to ignore him so he'll feel hungry enough to get up and find a job? Or does love mean giving him five bucks so he can buy either a meal or a bottle? Yes, it is our problem, because homeless people are sometimes in front of our faces with needs. No, we don't have to take care of everyone who comes across our path—just the ones God points out. And if we can't see through the darkness, it means we aren't always going to know "the answer," how to love when there's no beam of light on the path.

The heart is willing, but the flesh is weak. We want to love our world, but in the darkness we sometimes don't feel strong enough to love even ourselves. We must stay conscious and centered on God because the darkness can pull us inward, into itself. We can become involved to the degree that we are no longer carriers of light but have become a part of the darkness. We can become depressed and hopeless because we can't see any light, or angry when things aren't changing as quickly as we think they should or maybe aren't changing at all. In this black space, we can too easily forget that there's a world out there and that we still have a role to play. I believe that God's purpose in everything that comes our way, including those things we perceive as darkness, is to lead us to a larger capacity for love.

But too often we're looking only on the outside of a situation. Everything that presents itself to us has an external and an internal face. I can look at my loved one and see an alcoholic. Or I can look at my loved one and see not *just* an alcoholic but someone who has lost his way who needs a compassionate and unconditional expression of God's love. Of course, every scenario orchestrated by God between two or more people is not just for one of those people; it's always for everyone involved. When you commit to loving your world, no matter how that takes shape in your life, you're signing up for Life 101. Spiritual lessons are coming your way; make sure you're watching and listening.

I know a family with a child who has Down syndrome. On the surface, this would appear to be a kind of darkness we can only understand if we've been there. A darkness without hope, if you think of hope as a situation that gets better until everything is back to normal. No, this child will not get "better." This situation won't go away.

But this child is the family's teacher, sent from God, and once the family members began to recognize that, they were forever changed. Because he experiences life with such childlike wonder, no matter how old he gets, so do they. Whether it's the changing of the seasons or a nest of newborn baby birds in the backyard, the whole family celebrates what before they'd always taken for granted. He has always wanted to play football with the "big boys." When a professional team recently heard about his dream, they brought him onto the field one day and let him play. His family cheered like crazy. But they've always been his cheerleaders in life. If you talk to them, they wouldn't say they're in darkness. Without even realizing it, this family has transformed darkness into light.

This is the goal of learning to love: to redeem the darkness. And yes, it can be confusing. Sometimes you'll take a step forward, and it doesn't feel right. So you back up. The darkness will always be with us in one form or another. We will never, no matter how much light we walk in, completely rid ourselves of it. We're not supposed to. We're supposed to learn how to love in the midst of the darkness; how to love when we have no guarantee that the light in this particular situation will ever come on again; how to love when we have no one's footsteps to follow other than Christ's.

This is what loving our world is all about. Faith...in the God who created the darkness and who walks with us in it.

Ask Yourself

Who is God pointing out to you today? Who is in darkness needing you to light the way? What do you see as your role in walking with this person in and through the darkness?

How can you turn the light on so that it doesn't expose and cause shame but so that it illuminates the path to God?

To Do

Just for today, seek out the darkness and see what it has to teach you. Who do you find there? Don't run. Stay and learn. Move in a little closer. If in the darkness you find a person who needs you, assess the available roles and choose the one that fits you. Commit yourself to being in the darkness for now, trusting that God will shine his light when it's time.

Chapter Twenty

love's reward

I called a friend the other day to tell him I wanted to take him out to dinner to celebrate a special day, and would he meet me at—

"No, I don't think so," was his answer. "I don't trust you. Your love is suspect."

Ouch! Where was that coming from? I thought I knew, but I needed to probe a bit to make sure. Turned out I was right, he was blaming me for the pain he was in. I let him talk, listening and validating the best I could without getting defensive—not an easy thing to do. But loving him at that moment meant listening, even though I had my own hurt going on because of his rejection.

I had reached out in love and been rebuffed. That happens sometimes. I thought, *Okay, fine, you can sit alone on this special day. See if I care. You deserve it.* And when I was done licking my wounds, I decided to send him a card. He didn't deserve it, of course, but we don't love because someone deserves it. Nor do we love in order to get a reward.

Once we decide to love, we learn a lot about our motives. When we're not rewarded for our efforts, the real reasons for our loving surface. This keeps us on our toes, reminds us that we're loving not for ourselves, but for a bigger purpose. We're doing our small part to love in order to create a more loving world for everyone.

I have no idea how my friend felt when he got off the phone, but I'm sure our conversation must have confronted him with the revenge in his heart. Or at least the pain he needed to deal with. Love confronts. It's not up to us to make people listen to our love. Our task, or rather privilege, is simply to reach out.

Sometimes we reach out blindly, not knowing if our love will have any positive results at all. I remember a friend of mine, Carol, who watched a teen mom I'll call Jenny struggle to begin to raise her newborn son.

"It's not working," Carol told me one day. "She's simply too young. She can't give him what he needs. But I don't know what to do. She won't give him up. This is so hard to watch."

It went on for months. The situation was obviously getting worse: The mom dragged the baby around to teen parties and neglected many of his physical needs. His care plainly came in second to Jenny's social and emotional needs.

"I'll help you find a good home for him if you ever decide it's just too much," Carol finally told her, thinking of what was best for both Jenny and the baby.

A day or so later, Jenny called Carol. "I can't do this anymore."

The baby was adopted into a healthy Christian home where his needs are being met and his new parents are caring for him in a way Jenny never could have. In this case, Carol was rewarded for her effort to love.

Loving our world without the assurance that it's going to make any obvious difference is tough. We want to know before we put ourselves out there that we're going to receive a payoff. That's the way we're programmed. "Okay, God, today I loved Joe and Kathy and my obnoxious teenager and that goofy panhandler on the corner of Second and Yesler and that coworker who always steals my paper clips... What kind of a prize do you have for me?" But love is always a risk. We don't *know* there will ever be a payoff, and that is where we grow. When I say, "I love you," I have no guarantee that I'm going to hear "I love you" back. And so we hang on tightly to God's promise in Ephesians 6:7-8: "Serve wholeheartedly, as if you were serving the Lord, not men, because you know that the Lord will reward everyone for whatever good he does."

I can't write about this aspect of loving without admitting that sometimes I find myself thinking, *Okay, I did this loving thing, and no one even noticed. What's the point?* Sometimes when I drop my offering in the plate, I wonder if anyone on the pastoral staff saw me so that they know I'm paying my way in the church. At times when I organize an activity for the inmates up at prison, I want to make sure they know it was me. *See how loving I am, guys? It's me, the one who loves you.* Is that pathetic or what?

Obviously I need lots of work when it comes to loving without ulterior motives. But you know, writers aren't immune to the stuff they write about. Just the opposite. The stuff they write about is often on the cutting edge of where they live.

I'm learning that love is its own reward. Loving others is the most satisfying work we ever do. When we choose to reach out to love another person, with no promise of a reward in sight, that is God's kind of love. It's a rush like no other. (Not that we love for the rush. That would defeat the selflessness of the act of love.) I believe we were created to be lovers. When we're about God's work, the reward is inherent in the action of love, however it expresses itself. Pay attention. When we're loving, we are the presence of God in the world.

Ask Yourself

Who can I love today without needing acknowledgment for it? How can I love this person so that my actions or words are not the focus? Can it be enough that God is watching?

How can I continue to grow in letting love be its own reward? What steps can I take toward loving for love's sake?

To Do

Think about who is on your priority list today, who you want to love. This may be a person with a desperate need or someone who hasn't heard from you in a while and would be blessed by a simple contact. Consider how you can approach this person without fanfare, maybe even anonymously, with a reward being the farthest thing from your mind.

Chapter Twenty-One

the vow

You've had nearly twenty-one days to practice loving and to see whether loving your world is something you want to make your life's journey. It's a big decision…one that requires constant nurturing and a lot of help from the Author of love. After all, it goes against our nature (and all the teachings on codependency) to think of others more than we think of ourselves.

On the day that we decided to follow Christ we committed to do his will. Period. But we didn't really know what we were signing up for. Sometimes I wonder: If I had known, would I still have made the same decision? Or would I have run the other way—to the next booth to join Toastmasters or the Amway people? I've heard authors and speakers say many times that following Jesus is easy.

I don't believe it's quite that simple. While I don't believe Jesus puts a heavy trip on us when we decide to be a disciple, as humans we can do all kinds of things to make our discipleship heavy. We are experts at making our lives as complicated as possible.

But for Christians, loving our world is not really an option. It comes with the package; we just didn't know what the concept meant **at** the time. Oh, we might have said that we believed we should love others, but most of us didn't know (or even think about) what that looked like in everyday life.

I hope that in reading this book, you have begun to get the picture, and that while it's not as glamorous a picture as you might once have imagined it would be, it's the only picture worth painting.

You and I hold the brush to this painting. It's not *if* we use it, but *how* we use it that makes all the difference. We can love a little bit here and there, doing just enough to take the edge off our guilt: "Oh, I should be doing more. There's the hungry to feed, the sick and imprisoned to visit, the abused kids and homeless to take in, the oppressed and harassed to protect, the environment to care for..." It never ends. The poor and needy are always with us. And in one sense we are all the poor and needy. A little bit here and there will certainly help. It's the mission of the church to love. We can look at it that way.

Or we can love a lot. Every day. The same way we're expected to pray—without ceasing. This kind of loving has nothing to do with guilt. Or fulfilling the mission of the church. It is a personal and individual yes to God. The kind of yes that confronts, challenges, and transforms every encounter we have, that creates from the mundane an opportunity for all involved to grow spiritually and to draw closer to God.

The rewards of loving in my life, in your life, are immeasurable. When we decide that we are no longer going to make sure the world spins around us, our hearts are transformed. Loving always moves us outside of ourselves and gives us a higher purpose for waking up in the morning. Someone in my day, in your day, is about to encounter a miracle. Because of your decision to love, you bring the miracle of God's love to someone else. What a gift!

You'll soon find that loving your world brings tremendous freedom. You are no longer tied to old wounds of the past, to your rigid daily to-do list, to paranoia about being around certain people because of unresolved issues. And you didn't even have to join a twelve-step program to get here. You only had to choose to love. I believe this is the yoke that Jesus said was easy.

I want to make a daily difference in my world. Don't you? If you truly want to love your world in such a way that will make an eternal difference in yourself and in the lives of those you touch, I suggest you join me in making this vow:

> *I will be God's lover in the world, no matter how I feel*
> *at any given moment, no matter if anyone seems to*
> *notice. It is enough to know that God and I are a team,*
> *a majority, and that the world is better because of my*
> *commitment to be a lover in it.*

Welcome to one of the most rewarding journeys you'll ever take in your life.

If you enjoyed this book by
Gloria Chisholm, look for the companion book,
Forgive One Another (1-57856-311-9),
available at your local Christian bookstore.